THE MAREVA INJUNCTION
AND ASSOCIATED ORDERS

For Lady Hamilton

The Mareva Injunction and Associated Orders

BY
DAVID G. POWLES
LL.M., Barrister, Senior Lecturer in Law,
University of Wales Institute of Science and Technology

PROFESSIONAL BOOKS LIMITED
1985

Published in 1985 by
Professional Books Limited
Milton Trading Estate, Abingdon, Oxon.
Typeset by Oxford Publishing Services, Oxford
and printed in Great Britain by
the publishers

ISBN: Hardback: 086205 069 3
Paperback: 086205 203 3

©
DAVID POWLES
1985

Table of Contents

CHAPTER 1.   INTRODUCTION   1

Historical outline — the establishment of the
Mareva injunction — the basis of the court's
jurisdiction — the nature of the remedy — the
extent of the right of arrest in English Law — the
'trust fund' concept — the scope of the jurisdiction.

CHAPTER 2.   CONDITIONS FOR THE   13
GRANT OF A MAREVA INJUNCTION

Plaintiff to have a substantive cause of action within
the jurisdiction — plaintiff to show a good arguable
case — defendant to have assets within the
jurisdiction — real danger of removal or dissipation
of assets — just and convenient — presence of
defendant within jurisdiction.

CHAPTER 3.   APPLICATION FOR A   30
MAREVA INJUNCTION.

The time of application — type of application —
contents of the affidavit.

ACKNOWLEDGEMENTS

My thanks are due to Professor Kazuo Iwasaki, currently Visiting Professor at Monash University, Professor J. A. Tovar of the University of Madrid and Dr. D. Welp, Visiting Lecturer at University College Cardiff for their help in providing legal materials from their own jurisdictions. Also to my colleagues Robin Churchill and Andrew West for their assistance in tracing French and Swedish legal materials. Finally, to my wife, for reading the draft chapters and correcting many typographical and grammatical errors, and for her unstinting support throughout the preparation of the manuscript.

PREFACE

When the Court of Appeal decided in 1975 that an injunction could be granted against a defendant to prevent him from removing his assets from the jurisdiction before judgment, few could foresee the development of this new creature of Equity into the complex collection of rules and guidelines through the voluminous caselaw which characterises the Mareva injunction today. This development has been echoed, and has proceeded in many ways hand in hand, with a further incursion into the defendant's proprietry and possessory rights before trial by means of an injunction, in the form of the Anton Piller order, to enable immediate discovery of property and documents where there exists a danger that the defendant may destroy them or otherwise render them unavailable in the action.

Such incursions into the defendant's rights over his own property appear, in many ways, contrary to basic principles of common law and equity and little thought has been seen to be given in the judgments to the moral or ethical problems involved in such an incursion of privacy. Many may think the orders to be an unduly harsh and inequitable exercise of the courts' jurisdiction. Indeed, one aggrieved party has taken his complaint against such orders to the European Court of Human Rights. Such potential harshness and inequity has, however, been the subject of counter measures in that the courts have been at pains to emphasise first, that such orders should be used only in exceptional circumstances, and secondly, that adequate safeguards should be observed for the defendant's protection. The effectiveness of the first of these counter measures may appear somewhat dubious when it is considered that applications for such orders are before the courts almost every day. The second, however, has been pursued with vigour, the courts having jealously guarded against attempts to turn the remedy into a form of pre-trial attachment or, by its use, to adjust the law of insolvency in favour of the plaintiff. One major effect of the development has been to introduce into our common law jurisdiction a remedy, in many ways analogous to, albeit not completely equivalent with, the rights of arrest and attachment exerciseable as pre-trial remedies in many civil law, and in some common law, jurisdictions. In this way the new remedies can be seen as important factors in increasing the effectiveness of the common law and the attraction of English courts and English arbitration as forums of dispute settlement.

LLANVETHERINE
June 25 1985

TABLE OF STATUTES

OVERSEAS ENACTMENTS

RULES OF THE SUPREME COURT

TABLE OF CASES

CHAPTER 1

INTRODUCTION

In many jurisdictions the plaintiff is afforded the opportunity of arresting, freezing or otherwise preventing the disposal of, the assets of the defendant prior to the judgment so as to ensure the availability of those assets to meet his judgment if he is successful.[1] The plaintiff is usually required to give an undertaking to indemnify the defendant in respect of any loss incurred as a result, if the action fails, and the defendant can usually obtain the release of his assets if he puts up sufficient security to meet the plaintiff's claim.

In English law, arrest as a means of obtaining such security, is only possible within Admiralty jurisdiction[2] and, until 1975, a plaintiff in any other action had no means of preventing the dissipation of the defendant's assets, so that, in many cases, success in litigation brought only a hollow victory, the assets having been moved beyond the jurisdiction or otherwise disposed within it.

HISTORICAL OUTLINE

English law has not always been devoid of such remedies. In the seventeenth and eighteenth centuries a procedure known as "foreign attachment", a survivor of Roman times, was exercised in the courts of a number of cities and the right to arrest the goods of a debtor in satisfaction of the debt has been recorded from early medieval times.[3]

1. For a discussion of foreign procedures see Chapter 8.
2. For a discussion of this jurisdiction see p. 115 *et seq infra.*
3. For an early example see *Selden Society Select Cases on the Law Merchant* Vol. II 73–4. For a later account of foreign attachment see Alexander Pulling, *The Laws, Customs, Usages and Regulations of the City and Port of London* 2nd Ed. 1854 pp. 188–92.

Although this jurisdiction is long since defunct in England, the form of attachment currently practised in many states in the USA appears to derive from it.[4]

From 1352, until the nineteenth century (and into the twentieth century in some cases where the Crown was the plaintiff), an arrest could be made not of the debtor's assets, but of the debtor himself, and he could be kept in prison throughout the period leading up to the trial.[5] This power has, again, long since lapsed, leaving the right to arrest a ship, where the action is in admiralty, as the only example of a right of arrest or attachment in English law.

THE ESTABLISHMENT OF THE MAREVA INJUNCTION

The first buds of change, which in a few years blossomed into one of the most important interlocutory remedies available to a plaintiff, appeared in 1975 as a result of two *ex parte* applications which were considered by the Court of Appeal. The facts of *Nippon Yusen Kaisha* v. *Karageorgis*[6] and *Mareva Compania Naviera SA* v. *International Bulkcarriers SA*[7] have much in common. Both actions were brought by shipowners against time charterers in respect of non-payment of hire. In the *Karageorgis* case the charterers had vanished from the jurisdiction; in the *Mareva* case they were insolvent and again were outside the jurisdiction. Both defendants had assets in the form of funds in bank accounts

---

4. *Ownbey* v. *Morgan* (1920) 256 US 94 (US Supreme Court). W. Tetley, Q.C. in "Attachment, the Mareva injunction and Saisie Conservatoire", puts forward the interesting argument that the general power of arrest was never lost by the Admiralty Courts. See [1985] L.M.C.L.Q. 58. No such general power of arrest has sought to be exercised, however, since the eighteenth century, unless the decisions in *The Henrich Bjorn* (1886) 11 App. Cas. 270 and *The Beldis* [1936] P. 51 may be regarded as true examples of such a general power.
5. 25 Edw III, st.5 c.17.
6. [1975] 2 Lloyd's Rep. 137, [1975] 3 All E.R. 282.
7. [1975] 2 Lloyd's Rep. 509.

within the jurisdiction. In each case an *ex parte* application was made by the shipowner for an injunction restraining the defendant from removing any of his assets from the jurisdiction prior to judgment. In both cases the application was granted. In the *Karageorgis* case this was done on the basis that there was nothing in the statute, or in the Rules of the Supreme Court to prevent the injunction being granted, and that it should be granted to prevent the injustice which would be caused by the removal of the assets out of the jurisdiction. In the *Mareva* case, however, Donaldson J., (as he then was) felt unable to follow this decision because of the restraint on the court's power to grant injunctions echoed by Cotton, L. J. in *Lister* v. *Stubbs*,[8] which was not cited in *Karageorgis*, where he stated:[9]

> I know of no case where, because it was highly probable that if the actions were brought to a hearing the plaintiff could establish that a debt was due to him from the defendant, the defendant has been ordered to give security until that has been established by the judgment of decree.

Donaldson, J., did, however, permit an injunction for a very limited period for an appeal to be heard. In the Court of Appeal the problem of *Lister* v. *Stubbs* was considered more fully. As a result of that decision, two conflicting principles needed to be considered. First, that the court has unlimited statutory power to grant an injunction in any case where it is just and convenient to do so,[10] and secondly, that the court will not grant an injunction to protect a person who has no legal or equitable right in the subject matter

8. (1890) 45 Ch.D. 1.
9. *Ibid.*, at p. 13.
10. See the wording of the Supreme Court Act 1981, s.37(1), re-enacting The Supreme Court of Judicature (Consolidation) Act 1925, s.45 which in turn re-enacted the Judicature Act 1875, s.25(8). For the power to grant injunctions in the County Court, see County Courts Act 1984 ss. 38 and 39, Administration of Justice Act 1969, s.6. See also *Martin* v. *Bannister* (1879) 4 Q.B.D. 491. *Richards* v. *Culleme* (1881) 7 Q.B.D. 623.

over which it is sought.[11] On which of these two principles were the rights of a plaintiff prior to trial, who certainly could not, by any maxim of insolvency law, be described as a creditor of the defendant, to be determined?

The Court of Appeal decided in favour of the former by holding that a plaintiff who claims a right to be paid a debt has a legal or equitable interest in funds available to pay that debt even before he has established his right to the satisfaction of a court. Lord Denning, M.R. enunciated the new principle by stating:[12]

> In my opinion that principle (*i.e.*, that an injunction will be granted to a plaintiff who can establish the necessary legal or equitable right) applies to a creditor who has a right to be paid the debt owing to him, even before he has established his right by getting judgment for it. If it appears that the debt is due and owing—and there is a danger that the debtor may dispose of his assets so as to defeat it before judgment—the Court has jurisdiction in a proper case to grant an interlocutory judgment so as to prevent him from disposing of those assets.

The principle was confirmed by the Court of Appeal in the first reported contested case[13] and was shortly afterwards accepted by the House of Lords.[14]

THE BASIS OF THE COURT'S JURISDICTION

The basis taken for the jurisdiction to make such an order was section 45 of the Supreme Court of Judicature

11. *North London Railway Co.* v. *Great Northern Railway Co.* (1883) 11 Q.B.D. 30.
12. [1975] 2 Lloyd's Rep. at p. 510.
13. *Rasu Maritima SA* v. *Perusahaan Pertambangan Minyak Dan Gas Bumi Negara (Pertamina)* [1978] Q.B. 644, [1977] 3 All E.R. 324, [1977] 3 W.L.R. 518.
14. *Siskina (Cargo Owners)* v. *Distos Compania Naviera SA. The Siskina* [1979] A.C. 210, [1977] 3 All E.R. 803, [1978] 1 Lloyd's Rep. 1.

(Consolidation) Act 1925 (which substantially re-enacted section 25(8) of the Judicature Act 1873) which states:

> A mandamus or an injunction may be granted or a receiver appointed by an interlocutory order of the court in all cases in which it shall appear to be just or convenient.

The extension of the scope of the power to grant Mareva injunctions under this section did not, however, go entirely unchallenged. In earlier discussions on the scope of the provision it was suggested that it did not extend the jurisdiction existing at the time of the Judicature Act, but merely gave the court a statutory basis for the exercise of that jurisdiction.[15] Other authorities, however, suggested a far wider interpretation. Sir George Jessel, M.R. in *Beddow* v. *Beddow*[16] stated: ". . . the only limit to my power of granting an injunction is whether I can properly do so" and many other authorities support a wide interpretation of the provision[17] subject to the requirement that the plaintiff must have a legal or equitable interest in the subject matter.[18]

The acceptance of the wider interpretation did not of itself dissipate all doubts as to the efficacy of the Mareva type of order. Most such doubts were summarised by Bray, C.J. in *Pivovaroff* v. *Chernabaeff*[19] when the Mareva injunction, still in its infancy before the English courts, was struggling for acceptance in other common law jurisdictions, in this case, New South Wales. He pointed out that

---

15. *North London Railway Co.* v. *Great Northern Railway Co.*, (1883) 11 Q.B.D. 30; *Kitts* v. *Moore* [1895] 1 Q.B. 253; *Morgan* v. *Hart* [1914] 2 K.B. 186. See also *Doherty* v. *Allman* (1878) App. Cas. 728; *Harris* v. *Beauchamp Bros* [1894] 1 Q.B. 801; *Aslatt* v. *Corp of Southampton* (1880) 16 Ch.D. 148.
16. (1878) 9 Ch.D. 89 at p. 93.
17. *North London Railway Co.* v. *Great Northern Railway Co.* (1883) 11 Q.B.D. 30; *Cummins* v. *Perkins* [1899] 1 Ch. 16.
18. *North London Railway Co.* v. *Great Northern Railway Co.* (1883) 11 Q.B.D. 30.
19 (1978) 16 S.A.S.R. 329.

first, the weight of earlier and still binding cases militated against the introduction of a principle which deprived the defendant of the use of his property before judgment; secondly, to introduce a new jurisdiction similar to those operating in numerous civil law jurisdictions under the name of *Saisie Conservatoire* was a matter for legislation rather than for the courts; thirdly, existing legislation in New South Wales, which was identical to the English legislation, was not sufficiently wide to support the Mareva injunction, as it provided no more than machinery for the courts' use[20] and did not extend its jurisdiction beyond that which existed prior to the Judicature Act; and finally, that the legislature had already made provision to guard against absconding debtors[21] and:

> It would seem unlikely that an alternative process of summary execution in anticipation of judgment, available for unliquidated damages as well as liquidated debts, due and payable, should have been slumbering unsuspected for over a century in the interstices of s.45(1) and its predecessor and its analogues.[22]

Such objections did not prevent the continued acceptance of the jurisdiction in the English courts, nor its acceptance in most Australian and several other Commonwealth jurisdictions.[23] Within English law the jurisdiction has since been given the seal of legislative approval under the Supreme Court Act 1981, section 37(1) of which largely re-enacts section 45 of the Supreme Court of Judicature (Consolidation) Act 1925, Section 37(2) permits the court to attach conditions to the grant of an injunction where it feels it is just to do so, and section 37(3) authorises the court to grant an injunction on Mareva principles.[24]

20. See p. 4 *supra*.
21. Debtors Act 1869, s.35, mirrored in South Australia by Supreme Court Act, s.35.
22. (1978) 16 S.A.S.R. at p. 340.
23. See Chapter 8.
24. For a discussion of these provisions see Chapter 2.

THE NATURE OF THE REMEDY

In several of the early judgments the Mareva injunction was likened to the process of arrest, and Lord Denning prayed in aid the old remedy of foreign attachment as authority for the court's jurisdiction to grant such a remedy.[25] References to arrest (or *Saisie Conservatoire* in certain civil law systems), however, may only be used by way of analogy, and to equate arrest with the Mareva injunction is confusing, although it is still done.[26] The distinctions between the two types of action are clear. First, an injunction, whether interlocutory or final, can only operate *in personam*.[27] It does not operate to give the plaintiff any legal, equitable or other proprietary interest in the assets of the defendant. Such assets, therefore, are available to satisfy the claims of other creditors, whether their debt is secured[28] or unsecured,[29] or whether it arises in law or in honour only.[30] The plaintiff cannot treat such assets as security for his, as yet, undetermined claim or for his costs.[31] Secondly, arrest operates as a seizure of assets under a writ or similar authority which is patently not the effect of an injunction. Thirdly, an arrest must fasten on particular assets, whereas a Mareva injunction need only relate to particularised but

25. See eg.*Mareva Compania Naviera SA* v. *International Bulkcarriers SA* [1975] 2 Lloyd's Rep. 509

26. For a recent example see the judgment of Sir John Donaldson M.R. in *Tracomin SA* v. *Sudan Oil Seeds Co. Ltd. (No. 2)* [1983] 3 All E.R. 140 at p. 143. See also *Naval Consulate Assistencia Macpunas Maritimes LDA* v. *Owners of the Ship Arctic Star*, unreported 1985. The Times 5 February (Lexis transcript).

27. *Badische Anilin Fabrick* v. *Johnson & Co.* [1898] AC 203. *Bank of Africa* v. *Cohen* [1909] 2 Ch. 146. *Eastern Trust Co.* v. *McKenzie, Mann & Co. Lim* [1915] A.C. 760.

28. *Cretanor Maritime Co. Ltd.* v. *Irish Marine Management Ltd., The Cretan Harmony* [1978] 3 All E.R. 164, [1979]; 1 Lloyd's Rep. 491.

29. *Iraqi Ministry of Defence* v. *Arcepey Shipping Co. SA, The Angel Bell* [1980] 1 All E.R. 480.

30. *Cretanor Maritime Co. Ltd.* v. *Irish Marine Management Ltd., The Cretan Harmony* [1978] 3 All E.R. 164.

31. *Hitachi Ship Building and Engineering Co. Ltd.* v. *Viafeil Compania Naviera SA* [1981] 2 Lloyd's Rep. 498.

unspecified assets, *i.e.* those assets of the defendant within the jurisdiction.

It follows that where the injunction does not cover the defendant's assets *in toto* he is free to deal with assets over and above the amount specified in the injunction and may, unless the order otherwise specifies, decide which assets to leave untouched so as to satisfy the injunction, and which to deal with.[32] Where, on the other hand, the injunction applies to the defendant's assets *in toto* the practical effect is the same as an arrest. The same may be said of an injunction which applies to a specific asset such as an aircraft,[33] a ship,[34] or even a ship's bunkers.[35] In the case where the injunction applies *in toto*, however, the court has power to vary the injunction to permit the payment of other debts,[36] the defendant's living expenses[37] or his legal costs.[38]

Consequently the courts in applying the remedy have been jealous to guard against granting an application which would have the effect of creating a security for the plaintiff to the detriment of the defendant or his other creditors.[39]

32. *Z. Ltd.* v. *A.* [1982] 1 All E.R. 556; *Prince Abdul Rahman Bin Turki Al Sudairy* v. *Abu Taha* [1980] 3 All E.R. 409, [1980] 2 Lloyd's Rep. 565.
33. *Allen* v. *Jambo Holdings Ltd* [1980] 2 All E.R. 502, [1980] W.A.R. 51.
34. *Clipper Maritime Co. Ltd. of Monrovia* v. *Mineralimportexport, The Marie Lernhardt* [1981] 3 All E.R. 307, [1981] 2 Lloyd's Rep. 458.
35. *Sanko Steamship Co. Ltd.* v. *D.C. Commodities (A'Asia) Pty Ltd.* [1980] W.A.R. 51.
36. *Cretanor Maritime Co. Ltd.* v. *Irish Marine Management Ltd., The Cretan Harmony* [1978] 3 All E.R. 164; [1979] 1 Lloyd's Rep. 49 *The Iraqi Ministry of Defence* v. *Arcepey Shipping Co. S.A., The Angel Bell* [1980] 1 All E.R. 480.
37. *Ibid.* These and other cases appear to be a complete answer to Lord Denning's assertion in *Z. Ltd.* v. *A.* [1982] 1 All E.R. 565 at p. 562, that a Mareva injunction operates as *in rem* as a form of pre-trial attachment
38. *Ninemia Maritime Corp.* v. *Trave Schiffahrtsgesellschaft mbH & Co. K.G., The Niedersachsen* [1984] 1 All E.R. 398, [1983] 2 Lloyd's Rep 600.
39. *Per* Buckley, L.J. in *The Cretan Harmony* [1978] 3 All E.R. 164, at p. 170.

As Askner, L.J. pointed out in *A. F. Bekhor & Co. v. Bilton*:[40]

> The Mareva jurisdiction was not intended to rewrite the English law of insolvency in this way. The purpose of the Mareva jurisdiction was not to improve the position of claimants in an insolvency but simply to prevent the injustice of a defendant removing his assets from the jurisdiction which might otherwise have been available to satisfy a judgment. It is not a form of pre-trial attachment but a relief *in personam* which prohibits certain acts in relation to the assets in question.

More recently, Sir John Donaldson, M.R. commented:[41]

> . . . what (Counsel for the plaintiff's) order would achieve is a transformation of (the plaintiff's) status into that of someone who has power to wind up the (defendant) company— achieved indirectly, it is true, but nevertheless, achieved. That . . . would constitute a variation in the law of insolvency.

Further the right, and the assets concerned, need not be connected with the subject matter of the action, and a Mareva injunction does not in any way require the defendant to perform an obligation to the plaintiff, albeit the court's right to enforce such performance by means of a mandatory injunction is derived from the same source as that to grant a Mareva injunction.[42]

THE EXTENT OF THE RIGHT OF ARREST IN ENGLISH LAW

As has been mentioned, it is only in Admiralty jurisdiction that a true right of arrest pursuant to an action *in rem* may

40. [1981] Q.B. 923, [1981] 2 All E.R. 565, [1981] 2 Lloyd's Rep. 491.
41. In *K/S A/S Admiral Shipping* v. *Portlink Ferries Ltd* [1984] 2 Lloyd's Rep. 166.
42. *Astro Exito Navegacion SA* v. *Southland Enterprise Co. Ltd, The Messiniaki Tolmi* [1983] 2 All E.R. 725.

be enforced. This is considered in detail in Chapter 7. However, the assets of a defendant may, particularly where the plaintiff claims a right of tracing, amount to a trust fund in the hands of the defendant, so that a Mareva injunction protecting the fund is tantamount to an arrest.

THE 'TRUST FUND' CONCEPT

A series of cases[43] has sought to extend the 'ordinary' Mareva jurisdiction to protect assets which, in the hands of the defendant may be imbued with a trust, on the basis that they belong, in equity, to someone else. The effect of an injunction on such assets is, *prima facie*, to render them untouchable by the defendant or anyone else, and to leave them intact to enable the plaintiff to exercise a tracing remedy. The principle was summed up by Lloyd, J., as he then was, in *PCW (Underwriting Agencies) Ltd.* v. *Dixon;*[44] in saying:

> The distinction between the ordinary plaintiff and the case where the plaintiff is laying claim to a trust fund on the so-called wider ground, is thus clear. In the latter case the whole object is to secure the trust fund itself so that it should be available if the plaintiff should prove his claim. In the former case, by contrast, the plaintiff is not entitled to any security. The purpose of the jurisdiction, as is now clearly established, is not to provide the plaintiffs with any form of pre-trial attachment. It is simply to prevent the injustice of a defendant removing or dissipating his assets so as to cheat the plaintiff of the fruits of his claim.

43. *London and Counties Securities Ltd.* v. *Caplan,* unreported 1978. *Meditterania Raffinaria Sicilliana Petroli SPA* v. *Marbanaft GmbH.* unreported 1978. *A.* v. *C.* [1980] 2 All E.R. 347, [1980] 2 Lloyd's Rep., 200. *Bankers Trust* v. *Shapira* [1980] 3 All E.R. 353; *Chief Constable of Kent* v. *V.* [1982] 3 All E.R. 36. For a further discussion of these cases see Chapters 2 and 4.
44. [1983] 2 Lloyd's Rep. 197 at p. 202.

The existence of such a trust fund must be clearly established, however, before such an order will be made[45] and its extent fully defined.[46] Even where that is done, the nature of the order remains an order *in personam*, so that the court may, at its discretion, permit the defendant sums from the fund for living expenses and for the legal costs of defence.[47] It does not, therefore, create a true remedy of arrest.

THE SCOPE OF THE JURISDICTION

Although the Mareva injunction originated in, and in its early days was almost exclusively practised in, the Commercial and Admiralty courts, it is not confined to commercial transactions and, of necessity from the wording of section 45 of the Supreme Court of Judicature (Consolidation) Act 1925 and section 37(1) of the Supreme Court Act 1981, can be applied in any division of the Supreme Court. It has thus been applied in cases of personal injury claims,[48] transactions involving copyright[49] sales of a 'consumer' nature,[50] the proceeds of inter-bank dealings[51] and to domestic issues.[52] Applications for Mareva injunctions run, on average, at approximately 40 per month.

From two decisions on *ex parte* applications, therefore, has arisen one of the most formidable weapons in the plaintiff's armoury, at the interlocutory stage of the

---

45. Cf. *Trendtex* v. *Central Bank of Nigeria* [1977] 1 Lloyd's Rep. 581.
46. *PCW (Underwriting Agencies) Ltd.* v. *Dixon* [1983] 2 Lloyds's Rep., 197.
47. *Ibid*. The extent to which such a fund may be used to pay the debts of other creditors has never been considered.
48. *Allen* v. *Jambo Holdings Ltd.* [1980] 2 All E.R. 502.
49. *Faith Panton Property Plan Ltd.* v. *Hodgetts* [1981] 2 All E.R. 877.
50. *Prince Abdul Rahman Bin Turki Al Sudairy* v. *Abu Taha*, [1980] 3 All E.R. 409.
51. *The Theotokos* [1983] 2 Lloyd's Rep. 204.
52. *Barclay-Johnson* v. *Yuill* [1980] 3 All E.R. 190.

proceedings.[53] Whilst it clearly remains an order *in personam* and does not constitute an arrest of the goods, it operates to bring English Law on remedies more into line with that of most other jurisdictions and enhances English Law and English courts as a forum for dispute settlement.

53. As to the essential interlocutory nature of the order see *Stockler* v. *Fourways Estate Ltd* [1983] 3 All E.R. 501.

CHAPTER 2

CONDITIONS FOR THE GRANT
OF A MAREVA INJUNCTION

Although the cases establishing the remedy did not specify
any conditions precedent to the grant of a Mareva Injunction, subsequent cases have established a number of such
conditions, failure to fulfil any one of which will be fatal to
the plaintiff's application. Further, as the Mareva injunction is essentially an interlocutory injunction, the general
rules applicable to such will be observed and enforced. In
considering such conditions the developing nature of the
remedy must always be borne in mind. Earlier cases may be
superseded or otherwise become outdated and their authority, at best, confined to their facts.

1. The plaintiff must have a substantive cause of action
within the jurisdiction

The power of the court to grant an injunction is subject,
first, to the plaintiff pursuing a substantive claim for
damages or some other remedy, unless the injunction is
intended to be the final remedy, and secondly, that the
action must lie within the territorial jurisdiction of the
court.[1] It follows that unless the applicant for a Mareva
injunction can establish a cause of action within the
jurisdiction no relief will be available.

This principle was clearly established in *The Siskina*[2]
where Lord Diplock pointed out:[3]

---

1. *North London Railway Co.* v. *Great Northern Railway Co.* (1883) 11
   Q.B.D. 30; *Badische Anilin Fabrik* v. *Johnson & Co.* [1898] A.C.
   203; *Bank of Africa* v. *Cohen* [1909] 2 Ch. 146; *Eastern Trust Co.* v.
   Mackenzie Mann & Co. Lim [1915] A.C. 760.
2. [1979] A.C. 210, [1977] 3 All E.R. 803, [1978] 1 Lloyd's Rep. 1.
3. *Ibid.*, at p. 824.

A right to obtain an interlocutory injunction is not a cause of action. It cannot stand on its own. It is dependent on there being a pre-existing cause of action against the defendant arising out of an invasion, actual or threatened, by him of a legal or equitable right of the plaintiff for the enforcement of which the defendant is amenable to the jurisdiction of the court. The right to obtain an interlocutory injunction is merely ancillary and incidental to the pre-existing cause of action.

The facts of *The Siskina* are a good example of the application of this condition. The plaintiffs were the owners of cargo aboard *The Siskina*, which was owned by the defendants. The cargo had been purchased from Italian merchants, who had acted as shippers, for shipment from Italy to Saudi Arabia. The vessel was under charter to the shippers who had issued the plaintiffs with bills of lading marked "freight prepaid", and which were expressly subject to Italian law. The plaintiffs had bought the goods on c.i.f. terms and paid the sellers by means of an irrevocable documentary credit. During the voyage the defendants claimed sums by way of freight from the shippers. When part of the sum claimed was refused, the defendants diverted the vessel to Cyprus, off-loaded the cargo, and brought a successful action for its arrest before a Cypriot court. The cargo owners suffered considerable loss, both because of the delay, and because of deterioration to the cargo, some of which was stored in the open. The defendants claimed a proportionate amount of the freight they alleged was due from each of the cargo owners, although they had already paid freight under the bills of lading. Before action could be instituted by the cargo owners in either Cyprus or Italy, the *Siskina* sank and became a total loss. The vessel was insured in London, and the insurance money subsequently paid into the broker's account in England. The defendants were a one ship company registered in Panama and managed from Piraeus. The *Siskina* had been their only asset, and the insurance money now represented the only assets from which the plaintiffs could expect to be recompensed.

Although the plaintiffs' cause of action appeared to arise under either Italian or Cypriot law or both, they applied *ex parte* to the High Court to issue a writ against the defendants claiming damages and applying for a Mareva injunction to prevent the insurance money from being disposed within the jurisdiction or removed from it, and for leave to serve notice of the writ on the shipowners in Greece pursuant to R.S.C. Ord. 11(I)(i). This application was granted at first instance. The shipowners applied to have the order set aside on three grounds. First, that Ord. 11(I)(i) only applied where the injunction was sought as ancillary relief to a substantive claim. Secondly, that the claim for damages must be ignored, in which case the injunction could not stand alone. Thirdly, if the injunction was not ancillary to the substantive claim it would have to be the subject of the substantive claim itself which, as the application had been for an interlocutory order, it clearly was not.

These arguments found favour with the House of Lords who unanimously agreed that a substantive action was essential to support such an injunction. Here, it was pointed out, the plaintiffs had neither a legal nor an equitable right in the assets which would support a substantive action within the jurisdiction, in respect of which, notice of service of a writ could be served outside the jurisdiction. Nor would the granting of an injunction give rise to such a cause of action. Lord Diplock, commenting on the cargo owners' case, remarked:[4]

> In the instant case the (plaintiffs) have no legal or equitable right or interest in the insurance money payable to the (defendants) in respect of the loss of the *Siskina* which is enforceable here by a final judgment of the High Court. All that they have is a claim to monetary compensation arising

4. *Ibid.*, at p. 825.

from a cause of action against the (defendants) which is not justiciable in the High Court without the (defendants') consent — which they withhold. To argue that the claim to monetary compensation is justiciable in the High Court because, *if it were justiciable* it would give rise to an ancillary right to a Mareva injunction restraining the (defendants) doing something in England pending adjudication of the monetary claim, appears to me to involve the fallacy of *petitio principii* or, in the vernacular, an attempt to pull oneself up by one's own bootstraps.

This principle has been applied on several cases subsequently.[5]

An injunction may be obtained where the person against whom the order is sought is outside the jurisdiction and is "a necessary or proper" party to an action within the jurisdiction,[6] as where husband and wife are jointly sued in respect of an allegation of fraud and one of them is within the jurisdiction, whilst the other is absent but has assets here.[7] If the only issue before the court is its jurisdiction, then until that question is decided, an injunction may be granted by way of interlocutory relief.[8]

The legal or equitable relationship to the assets thus required is not confined to possessory rights, or rights based on the *locus standi*, to bring an action for monetary compensation against the defendant, and has been extended to grant an injunction on the application of a police authority over assets representing the proceeds of a crime, although the precise extent of this jurisdiction is not clear. In *Chief Constable of Kent* v. *V.*[9] the defendant was accused

5. *Obikoya* v. *Silvernorth Ltd.*, *Bergen Bank and Others*, unreported 1983, N.L.J. 803; *United Trading Corporation SA* v. *Allied Arab Bank Ltd.*, unreported 1984, The Times 23 July, The Financial Times 25 July (Lexis transcript). *The SLS Everest* [1981] 2 Lloyd's Rep. 389.
6. *R.S.C.* Ord 11 r.1(1)(j).
7. *Chartered Bank* v. *Daklouche* [1980] 1 All E.R. 205.
8. Civil Jurisdiction and Judgments Act 1982, s.24.
9. [1982] 3 All E.R. 36.

of defrauding an old lady by forging cheques drawn on her bank account. He paid the proceeds into his own bank account where they were mixed with his own funds. The Chief Constable sought an injunction to prevent him from removing any monies from the account before the trial, V being then on bail. The Court of Appeal granted the injunction, Lord Denning, M.R., on the basis that the jurisdiction was an extension of existing powers which enabled the police to seize goods[10] and currency notes[11] which they suspected represented the proceeds of a crime, and in this case the whole of V's account must be regarded as a trust fund and subject to the full rigours of the injunction; Donaldson, L.J., on the basis that the Chief Constable had sufficient *locus standi* in acting in the public interest, albeit the right only extended to money in the account which could be proved not to belong to V. Slade, L.J. dissented on the grounds that an injunction could only be granted where the police could show a right of seizure of the assets affected, as was the case with goods or currency notes or, in this case, a right to receive payment of the money in V's account traceable to the fraud, and here the Chief Constable had no right to claim such payment, even if they were to require the money as material evidence. Further, were the police to be granted such a right it would be over intangible assets which would not be restored *in specie* to the original owner, as was the case with goods or currency notes.

The decision, therefore, is not a strong one, and it is difficult to follow the reasoning of the majority and to reconcile it with Cotton, L.J.'s remarks in *North London Railway Co.* v. *Great Northern Railway Co.*[12] to the effect that a plaintiff must seek to enforce some legal or equitable right, the interest of the general public being, at best, a tenuous basis for such a right.

10. *Chic Fashions (West Wales) Ltd.* v. *Jones* [1968] 1 All E.R. 229.
11. *West Mercia Constabulary* v. *Wagener* [1981] 3 All E.R. 378.
12. (1883) 11 Q.B.D. 30.

MODIFICATION BY STATUTE

Two statutory provisions enacted since the decision in *The Siskina*, may affect the scope of the court's jurisdiction.

(i) *The Supreme Court Act 1981, s.37(1)*

Although this provision was intended to re-enact s.45(1) of the Supreme Court of Judicature (Consolidation) Act 1925, a slight change in wording has caused some confusion over the court's powers. S.45(1) set out the cases in which the High Court could grant "A mandamus or an injunction . . .", whereas s.37(1) refers to the court's power to ". . . by order (whether interlocutory or final) grant an injunction . . .".

This difference in wording led Lord Denning, M.R. in *Chief Constable of Kent* v. *V.* to remark:[13]

> The . . . words in brackets show that Parliament did not like the limitation to "interlocutory". It is no longer necessary that the injunction should be ancillary to an action claiming a legal or equitable right. It can stand on its own. The section as it now stands plainly confers a new and extensive jurisdiction on the High Court to grant an injunction.

He added that the restrictions placed on *The Siskina* were no longer applicable.

The approach received little judicial support. In the same case both other Lords Justice of Appeal refused to follow the lead to wider jurisdiction, holding that section 37(1) conferred no wider jurisdiction and merely referred to the machinery which the court had power to use. Donaldson, L.J. remarked:[14]

> These are wide words, but I am quite unable to see how it can

13. *Ibid.*, at p. 40.
14. *Ibid.*, at p. 42.

appear to the court to be just and convenient to make such an order, save in the enforcement or protection of a legal or equitable right or interest. Were it otherwise, every judge would need to be issued with a portable palm tree.

The full implementation of the *Siskina* rule in more recent cases would seem to confirm that the jurisdiction is unchanged by section 37(1).[15]

(ii) *The Civil Jurisdiction and Judgments Act 1982,*[16] *s.25*

The High Court in England and Wales is given power to grant interim relief where proceedings have been, or are to be, commenced, either in a contracting state or in a part of the United Kingdom where the court does not exercise jurisdiction, provided such proceedings are of a civil or commercial nature and are not amongst the classes excluded.[17] The excluded classes of action comprise revenue, customs or administrative matters[18] and proceedings concerning the legal capacity of natural persons, rights in property arising out of matrimonial relationship, wills and succession,[19] bankruptcy, proceedings relating to the winding up of insolvent companies or other legal persons, judicial arrangements, compositions and analogous proceedings[20] social security[21] or arbitration.[22]

The court may refuse to grant such interim relief where

15. *Obikoya* v. *Silvernorth Ltd. Bergen Bank and Others,* unreported 1973, NLJ 803. *United Trading Corporation SA* v. *Allied Arab Bank,* unreported 1984, The Times 23 July.
16. The Act implements the Convention on Jurisdiction and Enforcement of Judgments in Civil and Commercial Matters 1968 (Full Faith and Credit Convention), the Contracting Parties to which are the Member States of the European Economic Community.
17. S. 25(1) (a) and (b).
18. Sched. I, Art. I.
19. *Ibid.,* Art 1 (1).
20. *Ibid.,* Art 1 (2).
21. *Ibid.,* Art 1 (3).
22. *Ibid.,* Art 1 (4).

it is of the opinion that it would be inexpedient to do so, having regard to the fact that it would have no jurisdiction apart from the Act in relation to subject matter of the proceedings.[23]

The power to grant interim relief may be extended by statutory instrument[24] but to date no such extension has been made.

2. The plaintiff must show he has a good arguable case

In granting interlocutory injunctions the courts have had relatively little regard for the strength of the plaintiff's case, it being regarded as sufficient if the plaintiff can show that there is some case to answer and that his claim is not derisory or frivolous.[25]

In this respect, the Mareva jurisdiction appears to be an exception. In the first contested case, *Pertamina*,[26] the Court of Appeal described the plaintiff's obligation in this respect as being one to show a good arguable case. This, they did on the authority, first, of the general principles governing interlocutory injunctions and, secondly, the principles governing the application of R.S.C. Ord. 11 r.4, in respect of which the term "good arguable case" was adopted by the House of Lords in *Viktovice Hornia Hutri Tegrstvo v. Korner*[27] to define the obligations of the plaintiff in making it ". . . sufficient to appear to the court or judge that the case is a proper one for service out of the jurisdiction". The approval of this test was far from unanimous, however, some preferring other wording such as "a strong argument"[28] or "a proper (case) to be heard in

23. S. 25(2).
24. S. 25(3).
25. *American Cynamid Co. v. Ethicon Ltd.* [1975] A.C. 396, [1975] 1 All E.R. 504.
26. [1978] Q.B. 644, [1977] 3 All E.R. 324, [1978] 3 W.L.R. 518.
27. [1951] A.C. 869.
28. *Per* Lord Radcliffe at p. 885.

our courts".[29] Further, it has been pointed out that neither the general rule applying to interlocutory injunctions, nor the tests under Ord. II, are of direct application to the Mareva injunction, as the nature of the relief granted is completely different from that which may be granted on final judgment.[30] Nevertheless, the term "good arguable case" has been adopted as the correct test in a number of cases.[31]

What is meant by a "good arguable case" is not susceptible of succinct and exhaustive definition. Certainly the plaintiff must show that he has some sort of case to be answered, and his application will be doomed if no case can be made out.[32] The plaintiff does not have to prove he will succeed, either according to the standards of proof of a contested action[33] or where he seeks summary judgment.[34] He must do more than adduce the bare facts which support his claim[35] and must go at least as far as showing that he has a *prima facie* prospect of success,[36] albeit the standard of proof required for this will vary according to whether the

29. *Per* Lord Simonds at p. 880.
30. See the judgment of Mustill, J. in *Ninemia Maritime Corporation* v. *Trave Schiffahrtsgesellschaft m.b.H Und Co. KG, The Neidersachsen* [1983] 2 Lloyd's Rep. 600, at p. 604.
31. *Etablissement Esefka International Anstalt* v. *Central Bank of Nigeria* [1979] 1 Lloyd's Rep. 445; *Baharim* v. *Victoria P. Shipping Co., The Tatiangela* [1980] 2 Lloyd's Rep. 193; *The Neidersachsen* [1983] 2 Lloyd's Rep. 600. Also *Bidgood* v. *Setzer*, unreported 9 October 1984. (Lexis transcript). *Dynawest International Ltd.* v. *Margate Resources Ltd.*, unreported 9 November, 1984 (Lexis transcript). (See also the remarks of Slade, L.J. in *Rosenberg* v. *Sebarajah*, unreported 24 February 1983 (Lexis transcript)).
32. *Anstalt* v. *Snape*, unreported 10 May 1984 (Lexis transcript). Also *Re Multiguarantee Co. Ltd. (No. 1)*, unreported 1984. Financial Times 14 August (Lexis transcript).
33. *The Neidersachsen* [1983] 2 Lloyd's Rep. 600.
34. *Pertamina* [1978] Q.B. 644, [1977] 3 All E.R. 324, [1977] 3 W.L.R. 518.
35. *Bidgood* v. *Setzer*, unreported 9 October 1984 and see *Dynawest International Ltd.* v. *Margate Resources Ltd.*, unreported 9 November, 1984.
36. *Re Multiguarantee Co. Ltd. (No. 1)*, unreported 1984.

application is heard *ex parte* or *inter partes*.[37] In neither case should any attempt be made at the interlocutory stage to pre-determine the issue which will be considered at the trial[38] or arbitration.[39] Adducing a *prima facie* case is clearly insufficient. As Parker, J., commenting on the plaintiff's evidence in *The Tatiangela*[40] pointed out: "This establishes, I accept, a *prima facie* case, but it does no more. It does not show that the plaintiff has good, good arguable, weak or bad prospects or in any way reveal the quality of his case." The position was summed up by Mustill J. in *The Neidersachsen*[41] where he stated:

> . . . I consider the right course is to adopt the test of a good arguable case, in the sense of a case which is more than barely capable of serious argument, and yet not necessarily one which the judge believes to have a better than 50 per cent chance of success.

Such a case must be made out both in relation to the substantive point of law on which the plaintiff's case is based and, where relevant, in relation to the remedy he seeks.[42]

Thus, applications have been refused where the plaintiff's case was doubtful on many points and the defendant appeared to have a good defence,[43] where the plaintiff failed to produce adequate evidence that he was the party who suffered damage or that the defendants were in default,[44]

37. *The Neidersachsen* [1983] 2 Lloyd's Rep. 600.
38. *Ibid.*
39. *Ibid.*
40. [1980] 2 Lloyd's Rep. 193, at p. 198.
41. [1983] 2 Lloyd's Rep. 600, at p. 605 ; Applied in *Paramount Pictures Corp.* v. *Dimsey,* unreported 1 December, 1983 (Lexis transcript); *Continental Airlines* v. *Aviation and Tourist Marketing AG,* unreported 18 January 1984, (Lexis transcript).
42. *Dynawest International Ltd.* v. *Margate Resources Ltd.,* unreported 9 November, 1984.
43. *Establissement Efeska International Anstalt* v. *Central Bank of Nigeria* [1979] 1 Lloyd's Rep. 445.
44. *The Tatiangela* [1980] 2 Lloyd's Rep. 193.

where, although the plaintiff could show he had a substantive claim in law, he could not show a right to recover more than nominal damages,[45] and where the plaintiff was unable to adduce sufficient evidence to support his claim, both on *ex parte* and *inter partes* applications.[46]

3. The defendant must have assets within the jurisdiction

As a condition this is self-explanatory. The plaintiff's obligation to lead evidence of, and identify, the defendant's assets are discussed in Chapter 3. The assets may be in any movable form, and may include intangible assets, such as a chose in action, provided it gives rise to a right to have the proceeds paid within the jurisdiction of the High Court.[47] Thus, an injunction was refused over the proceeds of a letter of credit where the credit was payable in Greece.[48] The existence within the jurisdiction of an overdrawn bank account has been held to be sufficient evidence that the defendant has assets over which a Mareva injunction may be granted, on the basis that in commercial practice, such overdrafts are usually secured on other assets.[49]

4. There must be a real danger that the defendant will remove the assets from, or dissipate them within, the jurisdiction

The purpose of the Mareva jurisdiction being to preserve within the jurisdiction assets of the defendant which will be

45. *Dynawest International Ltd.* v. *Margate Resources Ltd.*, unreported 9 November 1984.
46. *The Neidersachsen* [1983] 2 Lloyd's Rep. 600, [1984] 1 All E.R. 398. Also *Bidgood* v. *Setzer*, unreported 9 October 1984.
47. *Intraco Ltd* v. *Notis Shipping Corporation, The Bhoja Trader* [1981] 2 Lloyd's Rep. 256.
48. *Ibid.*
49. *Third Chandris Shipping Corp.* v. *Unimarine SA, The Genie, The Pythia and The Angelic Wings, (The Genie)* [1979] 2 All E.R. 972, [1979] 2 Lloyd's Rep. 194.

available for the satisfaction of the judgment if the plaintiff is successful, the plaintiff has had to show, from the inception of the remedy, that ". . . there is a danger that the debtor may dispose of his assets so as to defeat the debt";[50] in other words, he must adduce some evidence that there exists a real danger that such assets will be removed from the jurisdiction of the court so as to leave him with, at best, the hollow victory of an unsatisfied judgment.[51] Alternatively, he must show that there is a danger of the assets being dissipated within the jurisdiction with the same effect,[52] which may include selling or charging the assets,[53] but will not include the payment of debts incurred in the normal course of business or lifestyle of the defendant.[54]

The extent to which the plaintiff is bound to prove an intention on the part of the defendant to defeat his rights on judgment, is not entirely free from doubt. The Court of Appeal in *Z. Ltd.* v. *A.*[55] felt that the plaintiff should prove the defendant would ". . . take steps designed to ensure that these (assets) are no longer available or traceable when

50. *Per* Lord Denning M.R. in *Mareva Compania Naviera SA* v. *International Bulkcarriers SA* [1975] 2 Lloyd's Rep. 509, at p. 150.
51. See also *Pertamina* [1978] Q.B. 644, [1977] 3 All E.R. 324, [1977] 3 W.L.R. 518; *Establissement Esefka International Anstalt* v. *Central Bank of Nigeria* [1979] 1 Lloyds Rep. 445; *Iraqi Ministry of Defence* v. *Arcepey Shipping Co. SA. The Angel Bell* [1980] 1 All E.R. 480; *The Genie* [1979] 2 All E.R. 972, [1979] 2 Lloyd's Rep. 184; *Montecchi* v. *Shimco (UK) Ltd.* [1980] 1 Lloyd's Rep. 1180; *Barclay-Johnson* v. *Yuill* [1980] 3 All E.R. 190. *The Neidersachsen* [1983] 2 Lloyd's Rep. 600, [1984] 1 All E.R. 398. *Manufacture du Pontis* v. *Wake*, unreported 2 August 1984 (Lexis Transcript). *Rosengrens Ltd.* v. *Safe Deposit Centres Ltd.*, unreported 1984. 19 July (Lexis transcript).
52. *Prince Abdul Rahman Bin Turki Al Sudairy* v. *Abud-Taha* [1982] 1 Lloyd's Rep. 240; *Faith Panton Property Plan Ltd.* v. *Hodgetts* [1981] 2 All E.R. 877. The Supreme Court Act 1981, s.37(3) uses the term "otherwise dealing with".
53. *Faith Panton Property Plan Ltd.* v. *Hodgetts* [1981] 2 All E.R. 877; *CBS (U.K.)* v. *Lambert* [1982] 3 All E.R. 237.
54. *The Angel Bell*, [1980] 1 All E.R. 480; *Cretantor Maritime Co. Ltd.* v. *Marine Management Ltd* [1978] 3 All E.R. 164, [1979] 1 Lloyd's Rep. 491.
55. [1982] 1 All E.R. 556.

judgment is given",[56] a requirement interpreted by Parker, J. in *Home Insurance Co. and St. Paul Fire and Marine Insurance Co.* v. *Administratia Asigurarilor de Stat*[57] as ". . . a requirement that (the plaintiff) must show nefarious intent", and by Mustill, J. in *The Neidersachsen*[58] as a requirement that the plaintiff prove: ". . . that the defendant will deal with his assets with the object, and not just with the effect, of putting them out of the plaintiff's reach."[59] The Court of Appeal in *The Neidersachsen*[60] refused to accept that the plaintiff need adduce evidence of the defendant's intent; it being sufficient to show that a real risk of removal or dissipation existed, Kerr, L.J. stated:[61]

> In our view, the test is whether, on the assumption that the plaintiffs have shown at least a 'good arguable case", the Court concludes, on the whole of the evidence then before it, that the refusal of a Mareva injunction would involve a real risk that a judgment or award in favour of the plaintiffs would remain unsatisfied.

This latter view appears more in keeping with the nature and purpose of the injunction, as if the removal or dissipation of the assets by the defendant results in the plaintiff's judgment being unsatisfied, it is of little practical importance to the plaintiff whether the defendant intended this outcome or not. Further, to require the plaintiff to adduce evidence to satisfy any more than a general objective test ignores the value of the order as an emergency measure and which may, of necessity, be made *ex parte* on very short notice.

Exactly what the plaintiff must prove to satisfy this

56. *Ibid.*, *Per* Kerr, L.J. at p. 251.
57. [1983] 2 Lloyd's Rep. 674 at p. 676.
58. [1983] 2 Lloyd's Rep. 600, [1984] 1 All E.R. 398.
59. *Ibid.*, at p. 606.
60. The judgment of Mustill, J. and the Court of Appeal are reported at the same reference.
61. *Ibid.*, at p. 617.

requirement has not been laid down except in general terms. It is not sufficient for the plaintiff to disclose that the defendant is domiciled or resident abroad,[62] nor will a bare assertion, unsupported by evidence, that the plaintiff believes that the defendant will remove or dissipate the assets be enough.[63] The plaintiff must lead evidence from which the court may infer, on the standard of a good arguable case, that there is a real danger of removal or dissipation.[64] In the case of an *ex parte* application such inference can only be made on the strength of the plaintiff's evidence alone, but at an *inter partes* hearing the defendant may adduce evidence to counter the plaintiff's allegation, and the court must arrive at its decision on the basis of all the evidence before it.[65] The mere fact that the defendant omits certain matters from his evidence or refers to them in indefinite or obscure terms, is not, of itself, a ground for weakening the defendant's case, as it is open to the defendant to choose what evidence he wishes to submit.[66]

The court will take into account any good arguable set-off or counterclaim put forward by the defendant.[67] Where the defendant is a foreign corporation the court will have regard to such matters as whether, under the system in which it is incorporated, it will be difficult, if not impossible for the plaintiff to establish the identity of the controllers,[68] or the location of the registered office or of the assets,[69] or whether judgment may be enforced against the company in the territory in which it is incorporated by virtue of the

---

62. *The Neidersachsen* [1983] 2 Lloyd's Rep. 600, [1984] 1 All E.R. 398; *The Genie* [1979] 2 All E.R. 972, [1979] 2 Lloyd's Rep. 184.
63. *The Neidersachsen* [1983] 2 Lloyd's Rep. 600, [1984] 1 All E.R. 398.
64. *Ibid.*
65. *Ibid.*
66. *Ibid.*
67. *Pac-Asian Services Pte Ltd.* v. *Steladean Ltd*, unreported 15 December 1983. (Lexis transcript); *Continental Air Lines Inc.* v. *Aviation and Tourist Marketing AG*, unreported 18 January 1984.
68. *Ibid.* See also *Anstalt* v. *Snape*, unreported 10 May 1984.
69. *The Neidersachsen* [1983] 2 Lloyd's Rep. 600, [1984] 1 All E.R. 398; *Anstalt* v. *Snape*, unreported 10 May 1984.

Reciprocal Enforcement of Judgments Act 1933.[70] It will also have regard to evidence led of the size and liquidity of the corporation's assets,[71] and whether the corporation has a history of defaulting on judgments or arbitration awards.[72] In all cases, however, the court will have regard to the evidence as a whole, and reach its decision after weighing all the facts it considers relevent. Thus injunctions have been imposed where the defendants alleged that they had substantial assets within the jurisdiction but did not reveal their private addresses or otherwise indicate where the assets were, whilst at the same time their business premises were empty and the company through which they carried on business had ceased to function[73] and, where the defendant, a foreign corporation, alleged that it had substantial assets but failed to adduce any evidence by means of accounts or balance sheets or through any officer of the company, of its financial position.[74] On the other hand, where evidence of the defendant's assets, and its history and policy of settling its indebtedness was put before the court,[75] and where the defendant was shown to be a bank of international standing and closely connected with the government of a large and prosperous nation, the injunction was refused.[76]

5. It must be just and convenient to grant the injunction

The statutory condition for the exercise of the jurisdiction

---

70. *Ibid.*
71. *The Genie* [1979] 2 All E.R. 972, [1979] 2 Lloyd's Rep. 184; *The Neidersachsen* [1983] 2 Lloyd's Rep. 600, [1984] 1 All E.R. 398.
72. *The Neidersachsen* [1983] 2 Lloyd's Rep. 600, [1984] 1 All E.R. 398.
73. *Prince Abdul Rahman Bin Turki Al Sudairy* v. *Abu-Taha* [1982] 1 Lloyd's Rep. 240. See also *Paramount Pictures Corp.* v. *Dimsey,* unreported 1 December 1983.
74. *The Genie* [1979] 2 All E.R. 972, [1979] 2 Lloyd's Rep. 184.
75. *The Neidersachsen* [1983] 2 Lloyd's Rep. 600, [1984] All E.R. 398; *Anstalt* v. *Snape,* unreported 10 May, 1984.
76. *Establissement Esefka International Anstalt* v. *Central Bank of Nigeria* [1979] 1 Lloyd's Rep. 445.

to grant an injunction, namely that it must appear to the court to be just and convenient to do so,[77] has been said to be: "The ultimate test for the exercise of the jurisdiction. . . ."[78] This will clearly be a question of fact in each case[79] but the courts have had particular regard to the question of the 'balance of convenience' between the parties[80] which, in the context of the Mareva injunction has frequently resolved itself into a consideration of the relative problems of the risk to the plaintiff of there being no assets to satisfy an, as yet, unproved claim on the one hand, and the potential loss and suffering caused to the defendant by a serious interference with, or total loss of, liquidity,[81] the loss of use of a vital business asset[82] or a major threat to his lifestyle, on the other.[83] The effect of such an injunction on third parties must also be considered,[84] and variations are frequently allowed to alleviate their position.[85]

The court will, where relevant, set the possible gain to the plaintiff against the possible loss occasioned to the defendant,[86] take into account the effect that realisation may have on the value of the assets,[87] and have regard to the possibility of the plaintiff enforcing a remedy more effectively in another jurisdiction.[88]

77. Supreme Court Act 1981, s.37(1).
78. *Per* Kerr, L. J. in *The Neidersachsen* [1983] 2 Lloyd's Rep. 600 at p. 169.
79. *Pertamina* [1978] Q.B. 644, [1977] 3 All E.R. 324, [1977] 3 W.L.R. 518.
80. *American Cynamid Co.* v. *Ethicon Ltd.* [1975] A.C. 396, [1975] 1 All E.R. 504.
81. *The Genie* [1979] 2 All E.R. 972, [1979] 2 Lloyd's Rep. 194; *Z. Ltd* v. *A.* [1983] 1 All E.R. 556; *The Neidersachsen* [1983] 2 Lloyd's Rep. 600, [1984] 1 All E.R. 398.
82. *Allen* v. *Jambo Holdings Ltd.* [1980] 2 All E.R. 502.
83. *PCW (Underwriting Agencies) Ltd.* v. *Dixon* [1983] 2 All E.R. 158.
84. See *e.g. Gallaxia Maritime SA* v. *Mineralimportexport* [1982] 1 Lloyd's Rep. 351.
85. See Chapter   *infra.*
86. *Henry Boot Building Ltd.* v. *The Croydon Hotel and Leisure Company Ltd.*, unreported 25 January 1985 (Lexis Transcript).
87. *Pertamina* [1978] Q.B. 644, [1977] 3 All E.R. 324.
88. *Ibid.*

6. The residence/domicile presence of the defendant

Although in the early cases Mareva injunctions were granted against defendants who were outside the jurisdiction, the question of whether the jurisdiction was limited to such defendants was considered at an early date by Lord Hailsham in *The Siskina*[89] where he pointed out:[90]

> I believe the truth to be that sooner or later the courts or the legislature will have to choose between two alternatives. Either the position of a plaintiff making a claim against an English-based defendant will be altered or the principle of the Mareva cases will have to be modified.

With one exception,[91] subsequent case law adopted and developed the second alternative, holding, at first, the jurisdiction could be exercised against a defendant who was present within the jurisdiction but who might depart at short notice,[92] and then extending the principle to all defendants, whether in or out of the jurisdiction, where there was a real risk that they would remove or dissipate their assets with the result that the plaintiff's subsequent judgment would go unsatisfied.[93] Any remaining doubt was removed by s.37(3) of the Supreme Court Act 1981 which states:

> The power of the High Court under subsection (1) to grant an interlocutory injunction restraining a party to any proceedings from removing from the jurisdiction of the High Court, or otherwise dealing with assets located within that jurisdiction shall be exercisable in cases where the party is, as well as in cases where he is not, domiciled, resident or present within that jurisdiction.

89. [1979] A.C. 210, [1977] 3 All E.R. 803, [1978] 1 Lloyd's Rep. 1.
90. *Ibid.*, at p. 829.
91. *The Agrabele* [1979] 2 Lloyd's Rep. 117.
92. *Chartered Bank Ltd.* v. *Dalouche* [1980] 1 All E.R. 205.
93. *Barclay-Johnson* v. *Yuill* [1980] 1 All E.R. 190; *Prince Abdul Rahman Bin Turki al Sudairy* v. *Abu-Taha* [1982] 1 Lloyd's Rep. 240; *Faith Panton Property Plan Ltd.* v. *Hodgetts* [1981] 2 All. E.R. 877.

CHAPTER 3

APPLICATION FOR A MAREVA INJUNCTION

1. The time of application

An application for an interlocutory order, such as a Mareva injunction, may be made at any time before or after trial.[1] Hence, the application may be made during ther interlocutory period,[2] or after judgment has been obtained, when an injunction may be sought in aid of execution of the judgment.[3] As a general rule, applications may not be made before a writ has been issued,[4] except in cases of urgency.[5] In such a case the court must be satisfied that the applicant has, at least, a cause of action,[6] and will usually require an undertaking from the applicant to issue a writ "forthwith", or "as soon as is reasonably practical", in which case failure to issue the writ as soon as it can practically be affected is a contempt of court by the applicant, and his solicitors may face a penalty for aiding and abetting the contempt.[7] It is desirable in such an application that a draft writ and endorsement should be submitted to the court or an undertaking given that the endorsement will be so drawn that it would have been appropriate to a writ under which

1. R.S.C. Ord. 29 r.1(1).
2. *Mareva Compania Naviera SA* v. *International Bulkcarriers SA* [1975] 2 Lloyd's Rep. 509.
3. *Orwell Steel (Erection and Fabrication) Ltd.* v. *Asphalt and Tarmac (U.K.) Ltd.* [1984] 1 W.L.R. 1097; *Danae Shipping Corp. of Monrovia* v. *TPAO*, unreported 7 March, 1984 (Lexis transcript).
4. R.S.C. Ord. 29 r. 1(3)
5. *Ibid.* See also *Re N (Infants)* [1967] 1 All E.R. 161.
6. *Cf. The Steamship Mutual Underwriting Association (Bermuda) Ltd.* v. *Thakur Shipping Co. Ltd.*, unreported 5 July, 1984. Lexis transcript, where it was pointed out that an injunction would not be granted at such time to preserve a possible future cause of action.
7. *P.S. Refson & Co. Ltd.* v. *Saggers* [1984] 3 All E.R. 111.

such an injunction would be granted, had it been issued at the time of the application.[8] The order will usually be entered headed "In the matter of an intended action between A and B".[9]

2. Type of application

Although, as a general rule, application for interim relief should be made by motion or summons, in cases of urgency the application may be made *ex parte*. This procedure is followed in most Mareva applications, as the defendant may, as soon as he is served with, or otherwise has notice of the writ, remove his assets from the jurisdiction as expeditiously as possible. As has been pointed out, the Mareva injunction "proceeds by stealth" to prevent the possibility that:

> By a few words spoken into a radio telephone or tapped out on a telex machine bank balances can be transferred from one country to another and within seconds can come to rest in a bank which is untraceable. . . .[10]

Hence the application may well be made at short notice, usually by junior counsel. The standard procedure to be followed requires the applicant to lodge with the clerk to the judge in chambers by 3.00 p.m. on the day before the application is to be made, the necessary papers, which should include the writ, the affidavit in support of the application and a draft minute of the order sought.[11] The judge in chambers will then hear the application at 10.00 a.m. on the following morning before he embarks on his published list.[12] Where, however, the matter is too urgent

8. *Ibid.*
9. *Ibid.*
10. *Per* Lawton, L. J. in *Third Chandris Shipping Corp* v. *Unimarine SA, The Genie*, [1979] 1 All E.R. 972 at p. 986.
11. *Practice Note* [1983] 1 All E.R. 1119 para. B 1(1).
12. *Ibid.*, Para B. 1(2).

for this procedure to be of use, the following procedures must be followed according to the time of day. Either, the applicant's advisors should attend on the clerk to the judge in chambers at 9.50 a.m. and lodge with him the papers specified above and a certificate signed by counsel, or by a solicitor where no counsel has been instructed, stating that the case is one of extreme urgency. The application will then be heard at 10.00 a.m.[13] Alternatively, the applicant's advisors must lodge the above papers with the clerk to the judge in chambers by 12.30 p.m. and attend on the clerk at 1.50 p.m. The application will then be heard at 2.00 p.m.[14]

Where, however, the matter is too urgent even for this procedure, the applicant's advisors may give notice to the clerk to the judge in chambers and the judge in chambers will hear the application immediately, interrupting his list if necessary. The applicant's counsel or solicitor must be prepared to justify the taking of such a course.[15] In a case of exceptional urgency, application may be made by counsel over the telephone to the judge in chambers.[16]

In cases of exceptional urgency it may well be impossible to prepare the necessary documents in time, in which case a draft affidavit should be submitted with an undertaking to swear and file, and an undertaking given, where necessary, to issue the necessary summonses.[17]

3. Contents of the affidavit

In making the application the plaintiff may well have to balance two potentially conflicting considerations, namely that the injunction, to be of use, must be obtained expeditiously, and that the court must be given certain information before an injunction can be granted. There

13. *Ibid.*, Para B 2(1).
14. *Ibid.*, Para. B. 2(2).
15. *Ibid.*, Para. B 2(3).
16. *Allen* v. *Jambo Holdings Ltd*. [1980] 2 All E.R. 502.
17. *The Genie* [1979] 2 All E.R. 972, [1979] 2 Lloyd's Rep. 184.

may be an initial attraction to the plaintiff in making statements at the time of application in the hope that they can be justified at a later date, but the fact that the plaintiff has to give an undertaking in damages to the defendant and any third party involved, and that the injunction may be considered in greater detail at a later *inter partes* hearing, may deter some of the more speculative excesses. Nevertheless, the question of what must be adduced may present a real problem to the applicant, especially where the matter is urgent. The application should have regard to certain guidelines laid down by the courts from time to time, bearing in mind first, that these are, with few exceptions, guidelines which will need to be adapted to the circumstances of each case, and not hard and fast rules, and secondly, that although, in theory, the same considerations will apply whether the application is made *ex parte* or is the subject of an *inter partes* hearing, far more evidence will normally be available at an *inter partes* hearing, and the burden of proof will be correspondingly higher.[18]

a. The applicant must make full and frank disclosure of all facts material to the application.[19] The importance of this duty was summed up by Slade, L. J. in *Bank of Mellat* v. *Mohammad Ebrahim Nikour*[20] where he stated:

> I think it is of the utmost importance that on any *ex parte* application for an interim injunction the applicant should recognise his responsibility to present his case fully and fairly to the court and that he should support it by evidence showing the principle material facts upon which he relies. Most particularly, I think that this duty falls on an applicant seeking

18. See the comments of Mustill, J., in *Nimenia Maritime Corporation* v. *Trave Schiffhartsgessellschaft mbH Und Co AG, The Neidersachsen* [1983] 2 Lloyd's Rep. 600 at p. 603.
19. *The Genie* [1979] 2 All E.R. 972, [1979] 2 Lloyd's Rep. 194; *Z. Ltd.* v. *A.* [1983] 1 All E.R. 556. *The Andria* [1984] 1 All E.R. 1126; *Manufacture du Pontis* v. *Wake*, unreported, 2 August 1984 (Lexis transcript); *Dynawest International Ltd* v. *Margate Resources Ltd.*, unreported, 9 November, 1984 (Lexis transcript).
20. [1982] Com. L.R. 158.

a Mareva injunction which, if granted, may have drastic consequences for the defendant, by freezing assets in this country which are not necessarily the subject matter of the action. . . . Nevertheless, no amount of urgency or practical difficulty can, in my judgment, justify the making of a Mareva application unless the applicants have first made serious attempts to ascertain the relevant cause of action and identify for the benefit of the court the principal facts that will be relied on in support of that cause of action.

Material omissions, or misleading facts in the affidavit, will generally prove fatal to the application, or constitute an important ground for discharging the injunction on the application of the defendant[21] and statements of opinion must clearly have some basis of substantiation.[22] Thus, where the applicant deliberately failed to reveal that his intention was to induce the other party to complete an intended purchase of a ship and then use the injunction to freeze a part of the price due to them, the injunction was later discharged.[23] In another instance, Mustill J., commenting on the applicant's failure to disclose that the other party was a company in a well established and respected trading group, pointed out, "Plaintiffs who seek Mareva relief will do well to bear in mind that the same obligations of candour apply to these proceedings as to any other form of *ex parte* application.[24]

b. The applicant must give particulars of his claim against the defendant, stating the grounds, the amount claimed, and setting out fairly the points made against the defendant in support.[25]

c. The applicant must give grounds for believing the

21. *Negocios Del Mar SA* v. *Doric Shipping Corp-SA, The Assios* [1979] 1 Lloyd's Rep. 331; *Z. Ltd.* v. *A.*, [1983] 1 All E.R. 556 at pp. 571.
22. *The Niedersachsen* [1983] 2 Lloyd's Rep. 600, [1984] 1 All E.R. 398. See also R.S.C., Ord. r.41 5(2).
23. *The Assios* [1979] 1 Lloyd's Rep. 331.
24. *The Niedersachsen* [1983] 2 Lloyd's Rep. 600, at p. 611.
25. *The Genie* [1979] 2 All E.R. 972, [1979] 2 Lloyd's Rep. 194.

defendant has assets within the jurisdiction.[26] It will not always be possible for the plaintiff to give the precise location and extent of such assets, but where possible the assets should be identified even if their value is unknown, and where it is known that assets are in the hands of third parties, especially banks, everything possible should be done to define their location.[27] Where specific assets are involved, the applicant should identify the assets in respect of which the injunction is sought, and the draft order submitted in support of the application should contain all the necessary details, such as, in the case of monies held by a bank, the identification of the banks and the branches at which the defendant has his accounts, together with the numbers of those accounts.[28] The amount of information available to the applicant will play a large part in determining the form of order sought,[29] and where insufficient information as to the whereabouts of the defendant's assets is available, the court may assist the applicant by making the appropriate ancillary order.[30] The court may also require the party against whom the order is made to submit affidavit evidence of the extent and location of his assets, and where this order is not fully complied with, order the party to attend for cross examination on the affidavit.[31]

d. The applicant must set out his grounds for believing that the defendant's assets will be removed from the jurisdiction,[32] which will, in many cases, be synonymous with showing that there exists a real danger that the assets will be removed.[33]

26. *Ibid.*
27. *Ibid.*, Also *cf.* Lord Denning, M.R.'s comments on the earlier unreported case of *MBPXL Corp.* v. *Intercontinental Banking Corp.* Unreported 1976; recorded at [1979] 2 All E.R. 984.
28. *Z. Ltd.* v. *A.* [1983] 1 All E.R. 556.
29. As to the form of the order see Chapter 4 *infra*.
30. As to ancillary orders see Chapter 4 *infra*.
31. *Buchmann* v. *Hayden*, unreported 28 September 1983 (Lexis transcript).
32. *The Genie* [1979] 1 Lloyd's Rep. 194, [1979] 2 All E.R. 972.
33. See Chapter 2.

e. The applicant should submit a full draft order for consideration.[34]

f. The affidavit must contain undertakings to indemnify the defendant against any loss occasioned as a result of the injunction, should the plaintiff be unsuccessful in his action.[35] Where, however, the plaintiff is incapable of fulfilling such an undertaking, the lack of the undertaking need not be fatal to the application if there are good reasons for granting it, and an injunction may be granted on the application of a legally-aided plaintiff.[36]

Where the effect of the injunction will be to put third parties to expense, the affidavit must also contain an undertaking by the plaintiff to reimburse such third parties all such expenses reasonably incurred.[37] This is particularly important in the case of banks. When the injunction has the effect of freezing the defendant's assets held by a named bank, the bank may be put to the expense of enquiring of all its branches whether the defendant has an account at any branch. This may involve several thousand branches, and such a "trawl" may cost the bank several thousand pounds.[38] Clearly the bank cannot be expected to bear such costs itself.

The applicant need not indemnify the defendant in respect of expenses incurred by him in identifying his own assets.[39]

g. The applicant must make the necessary arrangements to serve the writ, if it has not been served already, and a copy

---

34. *The Genie*, [1979] 2 All E.R. 972, [1979] 2 Lloyd's Rep. 194; *Z. Ltd. v. A.* [1983] 1 All E.R. 556.
35. *The Genie* [1979] 2 All E.R. 972, [1979] 2 Lloys's Rep. 194.
36. *Allen* v. *Jambo Holdings Ltd.* [1980] 2 All E.R. 502.
37. *Prince Abdul Rahman Bin Turki Al Sudairy* v. *Abu-Taha* [1980] 3 All E.R. 409; *Searose Ltd.* v. *Seatrain UK Ltd.* [1981] 2 W.L.R. 894. *The Genie* [1979] All E.R. 972, [1979] 2 Lloyd's Rep. 194; *Z Ltd.* v. *A.* [1983] 1 All E.R. 556; *Clipper Maritime Co. of Monrovia* v. *Mineralimportexport, The Marie Lernhardt* [1981] 3 All E.R. 664, [1981] 2 Lloyd's Rep. 458.
38. See the examples given in *Searose Ltd.* v. *Seatrain UK Ltd.*, [1981] 1 W.L.R. 894 and *Z. Ltd.*, v. *A.* [1983] 1 All E.R. 556.
39. *Z. Ltd.* v. *A.* [1983] 1 All E.R. 556.

of the order, on the defendant. Copies of the order must also be served on any third party affected by the terms of the order.[40]

40. *Ibid.*

CHAPTER 4

THE GRANT

1. The Extent of Jurisdiction

The power to grant an interlocutory or final injunction, as given under 37(1) of the Supreme Court Act 1981, may be exercised before, during or after the trial,[1] and in cases of urgency may be exercised before a writ is issued.[2] In relation to the Mareva injunction, applications have been granted before a writ has been issued on an undertaking by the applicant to issue a writ "forthwith" or "as soon as is reasonably practical[3] but an injunction has been refused where the applicant had been unable to show an existing cause of action against the defendant, and had applied on the presumption that the defendant would default on its obligations when the time came to honour them.[4] An application has also been granted after judgment to secure assets in respect of execution.[5]

In addition, an injunction granted before judgment may be continued after judgment so as to prevent disposal of assets of the defendant prior to execution.[6] This principle

1. R.S.C. Ord. 29 r.1(1).
2. *Ibid.*, r.1 (3). Also see *Re N (Infants)* [1967] 1 All E.R. 161.
3. *P.S. Refson & Co. Ltd.* v. *Saggers* [1984] 3 All E.R. 111. Failure by an intended plaintiff to issue a writ as soon as possible will amount to a contempt of court, and failure by his solicitor to implement the undertaking when he knows that his client has given it and is expressly or impliedly relying on him to implement it is *prima facie* a serious breach of the solicitor's duty to the court: it is irrelevant that his failure results from forgetfulness, dilatoriness or a mistaken understanding of what is expected from him.
4. *The Steamship Mutual Underwriting Association (Bermuda) Ltd.* v. *Thakur Shipping Co. Ltd*, unreported 5 July, 1984 (Lexis transcript).
5. *Orwell Steel (Erection and Fabrication) Ltd.* v. *Asphalt and Tarmac (UK) Ltd.* [1984] 1 W.L.R. 1097; *Daxnae Shipping Corporation of Monrovia* v. *TPAO*, unreported 7 March, 1984 (Lexis transcript).
6. *Stewart Chartering Ltd.* v. *C. & O. Management SA, The Venus Destiny* [1980] 1 All E.R. 718.

applies where the plaintiff has sought to enter judgment in default and would, under the Rules, be required to discharge the injunction before proceeding.[7] Robert Goff, J. in *Stewart Chartering Ltd.* v. *C. & O. Managements SA, The Venus Destiny*[8] stated that the principle, in such circumstances, rests on ". . . the inherent jurisdiction of the court to control its own process, and in particular to prevent any possible abuse of that process",[9] and added:[10]

> If the plaintiffs were unable to obtain a judgment in the present case without abandoning their Mareva injunction, it would be open to a defendant to defeat the very purpose of the proceedings simply by declining to enter an appearance. Such conduct would be an abuse of the process of the court; and in my judgment the court has power to take the necessary steps, by virtue of its inherent jurisdiction, to prevent any such abuse of its process.

In the case of a dispute which is to be referred to, or is in the course of, arbitration, the court has the same power to grant a Mareva injunction as it does for the purpose of, and in relation to, an action.[11]

2. The effect of sovereign immunity

Traditionally, under English common law, an organ of a sovereign state could claim sovereign immunity as a complete defence in the English courts,[12] albeit a modification of this rule was approved by the Court of Appeal so as to permit actions to be brought where the defendant,

7. R.S.C. Ord. 13 r.6.
8. *The Venus Destiny* [1980] 1 All E.R. 718.
9. *Ibid.*, at p. 719.
10. *Ibid.*
11. Arbitration Act 1950, s.12(6)(f) and (h). *The Rena K* [1979] 1 All E.R. 397.
12. See *Thai-Europe Tapioca Service Ltd.* v. *Government of Pakistan Directorate of Agricultural Supplies* [1976] 1 Lloyd's Rep. 1, and the cases cited therein.

although an arm or organ of government, was engaged in commercial activities, and the transaction involved was essentially of a commercial nature.[13] This application of restrictive immunity at common law will still apply to any transaction effected prior to the coming into force of the State Immunity Act 1978.[14] Where State immunity can be used as a defence, to a substantive claim, the court has no jurisdiction to grant a Mareva injunction over assets of, or held in trust for, a defendant within the jurisdiction.[15]

Since the State Immunity Act 1978 came into force, State immunity may not be used as a defence in certain circumstances,[16] the following of which may attract Mareva relief.

(a) In respect of a commercial transaction entered into by the state,[17] unless the parties to the transaction have agreed otherwise in writing.[18] A "commercial transaction" for these purposes means first, any contract for the supply of goods or services,[19] secondly, any loan or other transaction for the provision of finance and any guarantee or indemnity in respect of any such transaction or of any other financial

13. *Trendtex Trading Corp.* v. *Central Bank of Nigeria* [1977] 1 Lloyd's Rep. 581; *Hispano American Mercantile SA* v. *Central Bank of Nigeria* [1979] 2 Lloyd's Rep. 277. *Cf.* the views of Donaldson, J. in the *Ugange Co (Holdings) Ltd.* v. *The Government of Uganda* [1979] 1 Lloyd's Rep. 481.
14. 22 November 1978.
15. *Trendtex Trading Corp.* v. *Central Bank of Nigeria* [1977] 1 Lloyd's Rep. 581.
16. "State" includes "(a) the sovereign or other head of that State in his public capacity, (b) the government of that State and (c) any department of that government," but not any entity which is distinct from the executive organs of the government of the State and capable of suing and being sued. — s.14(1). An entity referred to above may claim immunity in an action in the courts of the United Kingdom if the proceedings relate to anything done by it in the exercise of sovereign authority and the circumstances are such that a State would have been so immune. — s.14(2).
17. S.3(1)(a).
18. S.3(2).
19. S.3(3)(a).

obligation,[20] and thirdly, any other transaction or activity whether of a commercial, industrial, financial, professional or other similar character into which a State enters or in which it engages otherwise than in the exercise of sovereign authority.[21] This third category, which appears to be a "catch all" provision, only applies to transactions of a commercial character which do not fall under the first two heads, and is the only one under which the courts are required to make a distinction between sovereign and non-sovereign acts. This distinction is not defined in the Act, but the wording of the provisions is in line with the approach of the courts in the pre-1978 cases,[22] where they had regard to the nature of the transaction rather than the constitution or organisation of the entity claiming sovereign immunity, an approach which has been adopted since.[23] Relief may not, however, be given against a State by way of injunction,[24] nor may the State's property or property of a State's Central Bank be "detained".[25]

(b) An obligation of a State which, by virtue of a contract, whether of a commercial nature or otherwise, falls to be performed wholly or partly in the United Kingdom.[26] This does not apply where the parties have agreed otherwise in writing, or whether the contract was made in the territory of the State concerned and the obligation concerned is governed by the administrative law of that State.[27]

---

20. S.3(3)(b).
21. S.3(3)(c).
22. *Trendtex Trading Corp.* v. *Central Bank of Nigeria* [1977] 1 Lloyd's Rep. 581; *Hispano American Mercantile SA* v. *Central Bank of Nigeria* [1979] 2 Lloyd's Rep. 1.
23. *Cf. Alcom Ltd.* v. *Republic of Columbia* [1984] 2 W.L.R. 750.
24. s.13(2)(a).
25. Ss. 13(2) and (4) and 14(4). Property will include money held in a bank account not intended or used for commercial purposes. *Alcom Ltd.* v. *Republic of Columbia* [1984] 2 W.L.R. 750.
26. S.3(1)(b).
27. S.3(2).

(c) In respect of proceedings relating to a contract of employment, including proceedings relating to an employee's statutory rights,[28] where the contract was made between a State and an individual in the United Kingdom or related to work to be wholly or partly performed there.[29] This does not apply where the parties have agreed in writing to the contrary,[30] unless the proceedings involved a point of law which requires them to be brought before a court in the United Kingdom.[31] The above exception does not apply where the individual is a national of the State concerned,[32] at the time the claim is brought or where the individual was not a national of,[33] nor habitually resident in, the United Kingdom at the time the contract was made.[34] Where, however, the individual is employed by an office, agency or establishment of the State maintained in the UK for commercial purposes the above exception will not apply unless the individual was habitually resident in that State at the time the contract was made.[35]

(d) In respect of proceedings relating to death or personal injury, or to damage to or loss of tangible property caused by an act or omission in the United Kingdom.[36]

(e) In relation to actions in respect of the enforcement of

28. See s.4(6).
29. S.4(1).
30. S.4(2)(c).
31. S.4(4).
32. S.4(2)(a).
33. For the definition of 'national of the United Kingdom', see S.4(5).
34. S.4(2)(b).
35. S.4(3).
36. S.5. In proceedings of the types enumerated in (a)–(d) brought in admiralty jurisdiction against the ship or cargo belonging to a State and used for commercial purposes, the statutory provisions will not apply where the State in question is a party to the Brussels Convention and the claim relates to the operation of a ship owned or operated by that State, the carriage of cargo or passengers or any such ship or the carriage of cargo owned by that State on any other ship. S.10(6).

patent, trade mark or plant breeder's rights belonging to State and registered, or in respect of which registration is pending in the United Kingdom, in respect of alleged breaches of such rights or of copyright by the State in the United Kingdom and in respect of the right to the use of a trade or business name in the United Kingdom.[37]

(f) In respect of rights in connection with membership of a body corporate, unincorporated association or partnership incorporated in or constituted under the law of the United Kingdom and having its principal place of business here, provided that body has members others than States,[38] unless the parties have agreed in writing, or the constitution of the body provides to the contrary.[39]

(g) In proceedings arising out of or connected with an arbitration to which the State has agreed to submit.[40]

(h) In respect of proceedings brought *in rem* against ships or cargo owned by the State being used for commercial purposes, or in respect of actions brought *in personam* to enforce a claim in respect of such a ship.[41]

(i) In respect of actions to enforce a State's liability in respect of value added tax, customs or excise duty, or agricultural levy, or in respect of rates levied on any property occupied by it for commercial purposes.[42]

3. Policy

The potential conflicts created by a Mareva injunction have led the courts to adopt, in considering whether to allow the

37. S.7.
38. S.8(1).
39. S.8(2).
40. S.9.
41. S.10.
42. S.11.

application, a policy of caution, which is manifested in the regard had to the basic requirements of the applicant's case, the balance of convenience between the parties, and vigilance in restraining applications which would stretch the injunction to the State in which it would be more injurious to commerce than helpful. As Lord Denning, M.R. remarked in *Negocios Del Mar SA* v. *Doric Shipping Corp.*, *The Assios*:[43]

> The Mareva injunction has proved most valuable in practice to the City of London and to all those who operate in the shipping world and elsewhere. But we must be careful that it is not stretched too far, else we should be endangering it. It must be kept for the proper circumstances and not extended so far as to be a danger to the proper conduct of business. So while supporting it wholeheartedly for all proper cases we must be careful that it is not extended too far.

This policy is also seen in the court's attitude to third parties and the requirement that the applicant undertakes to indemnify them.[44] Further, in any *ex parte* application, the defendant is always given liberty to apply so that, if he does not accept the injunction, or is unwilling to put up sufficient security to release the assets affected, he can always apply to have it discharged.[45] This right is being increasingly used, with the result that courts are faced with more detailed argument and evidence than in the past, so that the requirements of principle, where they can be accurately defined, must be met with greater precision.[46]

In view of the consequences of having to meet indemni-

---

43. [1979] 1 Lloyd's Rep. 331.
44. *Z. Ltd.* v. *A.* [1982] 1 All E.R. 556; *Searose Ltd.* v. *Seatrain (UK) Ltd.* [1981] 1 W.L.R. 894; *Clipper Maritime Co. of Monrovia* v. *Mineralimportexport, The Marie Lernhardt* [1981] 3 All E.R. 307, [1981] 2 Lloyd's Rep. 458.
45. *Ibid. Ninemia Maritime Corp.* v. *Trave Schiffahrtsgessellschaft mbH Und Co. KG, The Neidersachsen* [1983] 2 Lloyd's Rep. 600, [1984] 1 All E.R. 398.
46. See the comments of Mustill, J. in *The Neidersachsen* [1983] 2 Lloyd's Rep. 600 p. 602.

ties, and the possibility of the discharge of the injunction when more detailed evidence is put before the court on an *inter partes* hearing, an application for a Mareva injunction should not be undertaken lightly. Kerr, L.J. in *Z. Ltd.* v. *A.*[47] warned that:

. . . it is the duty of the plaintiff and of his legal advisers to do the following:

   (i) To consider carefully whether an application for a Mareva injunction is justified in the sense of being reasonably necessary in the particular case in order to achieve the objectives for which this procedure has been designed.

  (ii) If so, to consider very carefully what should be the extent of the injunction in order to safeguard the plaintiff's *prima facie* justified claim against a real risk of the defendant deliberately taking steps to avoid execution on a judgment which the plaintiff is likely to obtain.

 (iii) On the foregoing basis, in what way and to what extent the injunction should apply to assets of the defendant within the jurisdiction.

 (iv) To the extent to which the assets are known or suspected to exist these should be identified even if their value is unknown; and if it is known or suspected that they are in the hands of third parties, in particular of banks, everything should be done to define their location to the greater possible extent.

  (v) The plaintiff should consider how soon and in what manner the defendant can be served as expeditiously as possible, both with the writ (if this has not already been served) and the injunction if it is granted, and he should generally give an undertaking about service on the defendant as part of the order. Further, the plaintiff should consider on what third parties it

47. [1982] 1 All E.R. 556 at p. 574.

is meanwhile intended, and reasonably necessary, to serve a copy of the injunction.

(vi) All the foregoing matters should be fully and frankly dealt with in an affidavit supporting the *ex parte* application or, if it is urgent, a draft affidavit coupled with an undertaking to swear and file this forthwith.

(vii) The application should be supported by a full draft order for consideration by the judge, *i.e.* one which contains all the undertakings on the part of the plaintiff to which I have already referred and which gives effect to the appropriate injunction in terms which are adapted to the particular circumstances of the case.

4. The form of the order

The form of the order, and the extent to which it applies to the defendant's assets, will depend in each case on the way in which the plaintiff frames and substantiates his claim, and the extent to which the defendant's assets within the jurisdiction are known and can be identified. In many cases, insufficient information will be available at the *ex parte* application for an appropriate order to be made, and the order is frequently modified at subsequent *inter partes* hearings. This does not mean, however, that every effort should not be made to ascertain the most appropriate order when the *ex parte* application is heard, and

> . . . great care and precision are necessary in drawing the terms of such an injunction, so as to particularise the fund, the monies, the occupants, the goods or the other assets affected thereby and so as to avoid placing innocent third parties, such as banks, at the risk of being in, or committing, a contempt of Court if they should perhaps unwittingly commit a breach of the injunction. A Mareva injunction should by its terms be free

from doubt and should be clear, precise and definite in its operation.[48]

Although subsequent modification may remove gross injustices, the subsequent application may be time-consuming and costly. As Kerr, L.J. pointed out in *Z. Ltd.* v. *A.*:[49]

> Any subsequent hearing when adjustments of the original order may be made, should in my view only be regarded as a fall-back position. Thus, it should not be the practice (as I believe it to be at present, at any rate to some extent) that relatively little thought is given to what should be the appropriate terms of the order at the stage of the *ex parte* application, because it is felt that these can always be adjusted subsequently. Although this undoubtedly provides a crucial safeguard, it should not be allowed to overshadow the original application.

The appropriate order should therefore be specified in the application as far as possible, taking into account the following possibilities.

(i) *Order against specific asset*

The Court may make an order against a specific asset, such as a ship,[50] an aircraft,[51] a ship's bunkers,[52] specified items of machinery,[53] or goods in a named warehouse supplied by

48. Supreme Court Practice 1979 Para. 29/1/11/E. A more detailed note of the requirements is contained in the Current Practice at para 26/1/7.
49. [1982] 1 All E.R. 556 at p. 573.
50. *Clipper Maritime Co. of Monrovia* v. *Mineralimportexport, The Marie Lernhardt* [1981] 3 All E.R. 307, [1981] 2 Lloyd's Rep. 458.
51. *MBPXL Corp.* v. *International Banking Corp. Ltd.*, unreported 1975 (Court of Appeal Transcript 411); *Allen* v. *Jambo Holdings Ltd.* [1980] 2 All E.R. 502.
52. *Sanko Steamship Co. Ltd.* v. *DC Commodities (A'Asia) Pty Ltd.* [1980] W.A.R. 51.
53. *Rasu Maritima SA* v. *Prusahaan Pertambangan Minyak Dan Gas Bumi Negara (Pertamina)* [1978] Q.B. 644, [1977] 3 All E.R. 324, [1977] 3 W.L.R. 518.

a named seller,[54] whether such assets form the subject matter of the claim[55] or represent the defendant's only assets within the jurisdiction.[56] The security provided by such an order has been favourably compared with an arrestment of the subject matter in question.[57]

(ii) *Order against a specific bank account*

The court may make an order in respect of a specified sum of money located in an identifiable bank account.[58]

(iii) *Order against the total assets of the defendant*

The order may cover all assets of the defendant within the jurisdiction. As such, the order will not specify any assets of the defendant, but will have an ambulatory effect, attaching to all and any assets of the defendant as they come within the jurisdiction.[59] Most of the early orders were of this type, albeit they were not always precisely drafted.[60] The disadvantages of such a form of order are obvious in that the amount of assets frozen may well exceed the total amount which, on any argument, the defendant is able to claim[61] and the resulting total loss of liquidity may have catastrophic effects on the defendant's business and lifestyle.

54. *Manufacture du Pontis* v. *Wake*, unreported 2 August, 1984 (Lexis transcript).
55. *Ibid.*
56. *Nippon Yusen Kaisha* v. *Karageorgis* [1975] 3 All E.R. 282, [1975] 2 Lloyd's Rep. 137; *Mareva Compania Naviera SA* v. *International Bulkcarriers SA* [1975] 2 Lloyd's Rep. 509; *Siskina (Cargo Owners)* v. *Distos Compania Naviera SA, The Siskina* [1979] A.C. 210, [1977] 3 All E.R. 803, [1978] 1 Lloyd's Rep. 1.
57. See the remarks of Donaldson, L.J. in *The Span Terza* [1982] 1 Lloyd's Rep. 225 at p. 229.
58. *The Assios* [1979] 1 Lloyd's Rep. 337. *Z. Ltd.* v. *A.* [1982] 1 All E.R. 556. See also the 'trust fund' cases, *infra.*
59. *Cretanor Maritime Co. Ltd.* v. *Irish Marine Management Ltd.* [1978] 3 All E.R. 164, [1979] 1 Lloyd's Rep. 491.
60. Note the remarks of Buckley, L.J., *ibid* at pp. 168–9.
61. See the comments of Lord Denning, M.R. in *Z. Ltd.* v. *A.* [1982] 1 All E.R. 556 at p. 565.

Nevertheless, it may be extremely useful when the whole of the defendant's assets are insufficient to meet the plaintiff's claim, where the defendant is not resident or does not carry on business within the jurisdiction or when the defendant's assets cannot be readily identified, particularly when he may have accounts at several banks, some of which may be unknown to the applicant.[62] In many such cases the apparent injustice to the defendant can be overcome by the defendant himself if he applies for the release of any excess over the amount claimed by the plaintiff and at the same time discloses the location of all his assets within the jurisdictions.[63] Where it is essential for the location of the defendant's assets to be disclosed for the order to have any effect, the court may order him to make such disclosure, both in respect of property within the jurisdiction and outside it.[64]

(iv) *The "maximum sum" order*

This form of order, which is used in the majority of applications, specifies a maximum amount which the defendant may not remove from the jurisdiction, leaving him free to deal with his assets in so far as they exceed the sum specified.[65] This sum should represent the maximum amount which the plaintiff may reasonably hope to recover, taking into account liquidated and unliquidated claims; if the amount specified grossly exceeds this severe injustice may result to the defendant in having frozen assets which would never be needed to satisfy the judgment whatever the degree of the plaintiff's success. A striking recent example may be found where the order froze £25,000 in a specific

---

62. *Ibid.*
63. *Ibid.*
64. *Ibid.* Also *A. J. Bekhor & Co. Ltd.* v. *Bilton* [1981] Q.B. 29, [1981] 2 All E.R. 565, [1981] 2 Lloyd's Rep. 491; *PCW (Underwriting Agencies) Ltd.* v. *Dixon* [1983] 2 All E.R. 158. For a discussion of ancillary orders see p. 60 *et seq infra.*
65. *Z. Ltd.* v. *A.* [1982] 1 All E.R. 556.

bank account, albeit, as was later shown at an *inter partes* hearing, the maximum amount which the plaintiffs could reasonably hope to recover was £2,000.[66]

The main problem posed by such orders is the position of third parties, especially of banks, who are in possession of the defendant's assets. If a defendant has several bank accounts and an order is made preventing him from removing any sum up to a maximum of £X from the jurisdiction, how can any bank at which an account is kept tell whether, in honouring cheques drawn by the defendant, or permitting withdrawals, it is not abetting a contempt? Only an appropriate form of order can overcome this problem, and it has been suggested[67] that, as the main purpose of the order is to impose a general restraint on the defendant, the order should, in the first paragraph, restrain the defendant in general terms from removing the maximum sum specified, but should qualify this in the second paragraph by stating that as far as bank accounts are concerned the defendant is not to be entitled to draw on any of them except to the extent to which any of them exceed the maximum sum referred to in the first paragraph.

An order in maximum sum form should not affect third parties, particularly banks, in respect of items left with them for safe keeping, and indeed a bank may be quite ignorant of what may be left in one of its safe deposits, nor should it affect such things as shares or title deeds, as banks cannot reasonably be expected to assess the value of these so as to ascertain to what extent, if at all, they may be subject to the order.[68] The order should also contain provision enabling a bank to exercise any right of set-off which may accrue to it and which may involve money in an account subject to the order.[69]

66. *Sadiq* v. *Khan* unreported 8 September, 1983 (Lexis transcript).
67. *Per* Kerr L.J. in *Z. Ltd.* v. *A.* [1982] 1 All E.R. 556, at pp. 575–6.
68. *Ibid.*
69. *Oceanica Castelana Armadora SA* v. *Mineralimportexport Ataka Navigation Inc.*, *The Theotokos* [1983] 2 Lloyd's Rep. 204.

Particular problems may arise in respect of joint accounts and accounts in a foreign currency. In the former case it may be impossible for a bank to know how much belongs to each account holder, and the other holders may not be defendants in the action and therefore not subject to the injunction. Consequently orders should exclude joint accounts except in cases where their specific inclusion is justified, in which case the other account holders should be served with a copy of the order.[70] As regards accounts in a currency other than that expressed in the order, there is no reason to exclude or otherwise make special provision in the order, as the bank can convert the amount standing to credit into the currency specified in the order at the current buying rate, and put a stop on the account except in so far as it exceeds the maximum sum.[71]

The position was summarised by Kerr, L.J. in *Z. Ltd.* v. *A.* as follows:[72]

> In my view the first part of the order should bind the defendant in relation to his assets generally to the extent to which this is reasonably necessary. Secondly, where it is intended to serve a copy of the order on third parties the order should provide expressly to what extent assets in the hands of third parties are affected by the generality of the first part of the order. Thus, this part of the order should make it clear that, so far as concerns the assets in the hands of third parties, the generality of the order should only apply to such assets in so far as they are identified or referred to specifically but not otherwise. Accordingly, in relation to banks the terms of the order should in general only apply to accounts held by any bank *referred to in the order and only to the extent specified in the order*. (Emphasis supplied).

(v) *Expenses* etc.

In the case of an order covering the defendant's total assets,

70. *Z. Ltd.* v. *A.* [1982] 1 All E.R. 556.
71. *Ibid.*
72. *Ibid.*, at p. 577.

and in some cases where a maximum sum order is involved, it will be essential to provide that the defendant be permitted to draw certain sums which would otherwise be in breach of the injunction, otherwise the effect of the order would be to leave him totally destitute at a time when no claim has been proved against him. A reasonable sum will therefore be allowed for living expenses,[73] and in calculating the amount of such sum, account should be taken of the defendant's wealth and social position and of his normal life-style.[74] A defendant cannot be expected, for example, to give up his home, or take his children away from public school, when his liability has not been proved or assessed.[75] An amount may also be allowed to enable a defendant to defray day to day business expenses where these cannot be met without otherwise violating the order.[76] Sums necessary to cover legal costs will be allowed in all cases where the effect of the injunction would otherwise leave the defendant unable to give appropriate instructions for his defence.[77]

(vi) *Undertakings*

The undertakings given by the applicant to indemnify the defendant if the claim proves unsuccessful, and third parties in respect of costs reasonably incurred by them in complying with the order, should usually be contained in the order.[78]

---

73. *Ibid.* Also *A. J. Bekhor & Co. Ltd.* v. *Bilton* [1981] Q.B. 293, [1981] 2 All E.R. 565, [1981] 2 Lloyd's Rep. 491; *PCW (Underwriting Agencies) Ltd.* v. *Dixon* [1983] 2 All E.R. 158.
74. *PCW (Underwriting Agencies) Ltd.* v. *Dixon* [1983] 2 All E.R. 158.
75. *Ibid.*
76. *Purcell* v. *Geoprojects SARL*, unreported 21 July, 1983 (Lexis transcript).
77. *Z. Ltd.* v. *A.* [1982] 1 All E.R. 556; *PCW (Underwriting Agencies) Ltd.* v. *Dixon* [1983] 2 All E.R. 158.
78. *Searose Ltd.* v. *Seatrain UK Ltd.* [1981] 1 W.L.R. 894; *Z Ltd.* v. *A.* [1982] 1 All E.R. 556.

(vii) *Service*

The order should contain the names and addresses of all parties on whom copies of the order are to be served.[79]

(viii) *Return days*

Although the defendant will always be given liberty to apply, it is not thought advisable to specify a return day in the order except in exceptional circumstances, as first, it may tend to lessen the diligence which should be applied in ensuring, as far as possible, that the appropriate order is made in the first application, and secondly, to do so would inevitably lead to congestion in the courts. There will be many occasions when a further hearing will need to be adjourned, especially where the defendant is outside the jurisdiction, which will take up more unnecessary time if a return day is specified.[80]

5. The subject matter of the order

A Mareva injunction may be granted over any assets of the defendant within the jurisdiction,[81] and for these purposes assets will include both tangible and intangible assets, *i.e.*, all forms of chattels, as well as choses in action.[82] An order may be made preventing the defendant from disposing of, dealing with or charging real property[83] or from disposing of the proceeds of the sale of property.[84] Realty may be comprised in the assets subject to a maximum sum order.[85]

79. *Ibid.*
80. *Z. Ltd.* v. *A.* [1982] 1 All E.R. 556.
81. The crucial test is one of ownership; reputed ownership or possession do not appear to be relevant. *The Theotokos* [1983] 2 Lloyd's Rep. 204.
82. *CBS (UK) Ltd.* v. *Lambert* [1982] 3 All E.R. 347.
83. *Fearman Ltd.* v. *The Dorset Corporation*, unreported 12 July, 1984 (Lexis transcript).
84. *Millersons Investment Co. Ltd.* v. *Yorkas*, unreported 12 March, 1984 (Lexis transcript).
85. *Fearman Ltd.* v. *The Dorset Corporation*, unreported 12 July, 1984.

Where an injunction affects the disposal of realty it does not constitute a registrable charge.[86]

Where the order involves a maximum sum it usually specifies that the defendant must not dispose of assets save to the extent that there remains within the jurisdiction "free and unencumbered" assets to the value of the maximum sum. In deciding whether the defendant has complied with this requirement regard must be had to the value of the defendant's equity in any asset which is subject to a charge or encumbrance. It does not mean that the defendant may not "encumber" his assets, in the sense of making them available to satisfy other liabilities should they arise and thereby using them to provide security, as it will always be open to the defendant to "free" them by discharging the debt.[87] Problems have arisen in relation to:

(i) *Letters of credit etc.*

Where the defendant is a beneficiary under a letter of credit it is clear that the courts will not interfere with the performance of the bank's obligation except in cases of fraud,[88] as the security given by such a letter puts the beneficiary in the same position as if he had been entitled to cash. The rule also applies to bank guarantees and performance bonds.[89] Consequently a Mareva injunction

86. *Stockler* v. *Fourways Estates Ltd.*, [1983] 3 All E.R. 501.
87. *Stockler* v. *Wroughton*, unreported 17 July, 1983 (Lexis transcript).
88. *Edward Owen Engineering Ltd.* v. *Barclays Bank* [1978] 1 Q.B. 159, *RD. Harbottle (Mercantile) Ltd.* v. *National Westminster Bank Ltd.* [1978] Q.B. 146, [1977] 2 All E.R. 862; *Howe Richardson Scale Co. Ltd.* v. *Polimex-Cekop and National Westminster Bank Ltd.* [1978] Lloyd's Rep. 161; *United Trading Corp. SA* v. *Allied Arab Bank Ltd*, unreported 17 July, 1984 (Lexis transcript); *Intraco* v. *Notis Shipping Corp, The Bhoja Trader* [1981] 2 Lloyd's Rep. 256. The Times 28 Feb. (Lexis transcript); *Potton Homes Ltd.* v. *Coleman Contractors Ltd.*, unreported 1984. The Times, 28 February (Lexis transcript).
89. *United Trading Corp. SA* v. *Allied Arab Bank Ltd.*, unreported 1984, The Times 23 July 1984; *Edward Owen Engineering Ltd.* v. *Barclays Bank* [1978] 1 Q.B. 159.

will not be granted in relation to the beneficiary's right to enforce such an obligation.

A Mareva injunction may, however, be granted over the proceeds of such a letter, guarantee or bond[90] and the order can be made before payment falls due in contemplation of money being paid to the defendant.[91] An injunction can only be granted, however, where money to be paid under the letter, guarantee or bond is payable within the jurisdiction, otherwise there will be nothing for the injunction to bite on.[92] Thus in *Intraco Ltd.* v. *Notis Shipping Corp., The Bhoja Trader*[93] an injunction was refused over a sum payable under a guarantee by a London Bank as, under the terms of the guarantee, the money was payable in Piraeus.

(ii) *Bills of Exchange*

Some of the above considerations will apply to bills of exchange as there would seem to be no ground for preventing payment to a holder in due course.[94]

As between two immediate parties to a bill there may be circumstances where the payee will be restrained from removing the assets arising from payment out of the jurisdiction, especially in the case of a foreign bill, but all the requirements for a Mareva injunction must be satisfied.[95] The existence of a counterclaim by the other party, as when the drawer counterclaimed against the payee, will not, *per se*, be a sufficient ground for an injunction or a stay of execution.[96]

90. *The Bhoja Trader* [1981] 2 Lloyd's Rep. 256.
91. *Ibid.*
92. *Ibid.*
93. *Ibid.*
94. Bills of Exchange Act 1882, Ss. 29 and 38. See also *Z. Ltd.* v. *A.* [1982] 1 All E.R. 556.
95. *Montecchi v. Shimco (UK) Ltd.* [1980] 1 Lloyd's Rep. 50.
96. *Ibid.*

(iii) *Assigned debts*

Where the defendant has made a *bona fide* assignment for value of a debt due to him at a time before a Mareva injunction is granted against him, the injunction will not cover the proceeds recovered in respect of the debt,[97] as until the injunction is effective, the defendant is free to deal with his property as he wishes.[98]

(iv) *Assets subject to a constructive trust*

The concept that property in the defendant's hands could be regarded as a trust fund and "frozen" by means of a Mareva injunction so that it will remain intact and identifiable in the hands of the defendant or a third party, was first recognised in two unreported cases (in 1978) *London and Counties Securities Ltd.* v. *Caplan* and *Meditterania Raffinaria Sicilliana Petroli Spa* v. *Marbanaft GmbH*.[99] In the latter case the plaintiffs wished to trace a sum of money paid into a bank account as a result of a mistake in a commercial transaction. In agreeing to grant a Mareva injunction preventing its disposal by the bank, together with an order for discovery, Templeman, L.J. commented:[1]

> It is a strong order, but the plaintiff's case is that here is a trust fund of (the money). This has disappeared; and the gentlemen against whom the orders are sought may be able to give information as to where it is and who is in charge of it. A court of equity has never hesitated to use the strongest powers to protect and preserve a trust fund in interlocutory proceedings on the basis that, if the trust fund disappears by the time the action comes to trial, equity will have been invoked in vain.

97. *Pharoas Plywood Ltd.* v. *Allied Wood Products Co. (Pte) Ltd.*, Lloyd's Maritime Newsletter, Issue 7, 1980.
98. *Ibid*. See also *Ellerman Lines Ltd.* v. *Lancaster Maritime Co. Ltd.*, The *Lancaster* [1980] 2 Lloyd's Rep. 497.
99. Cited in *A.* v. *C.* [1980] 2 All E.R. 347.
 1. *Ibid*.

This statement was relied upon by Robert Goff, J. in *A.* v. *C.*[2] when he applied the remedy to a sum of money deposited at the bank when the plaintiff claimed that this money represented the proceeds of a fraud of which he was the victim. A similar order was made in *Bankers Trust Co.* v. *Shapira*[3] where a bank was completely innocent. The Court of Appeal was prepared to treat this as a trust fund and restrain its disposal at the same time making an order for discovery against the bank, the plaintiffs having undertaken to indemnify the bank for the costs of complying with the order.

A rather different situation was considered in *Chief Constable of Kent* v. *V.*[4] where the Chief Constable sought an order in respect of money in a bank account in the name of the accused, some of which, it was alleged, represented the proceeds of forgery. The Court of Appeal again granted an injunction, albeit no clear statement of principle emerged. The majority view though, took account of the Chief Constable's position as a custodian of law and order and in that capacity could regard the money in the account, or at least as much of it as could be attributed to the forgeries, as a trust fund.

The effect of these cases was considered by Lloyd, J. in *PCW (Underwriting Agencies)* v. *Dixon*[5] where he stated:[6]

> The distinction between the ordinary Mareva plaintiff . . . and the case where the plaintiff is laying claim to a trust fund on the so-called wider ground, is thus clear. In the latter case the whole object is to secure the trust fund itself so that it should be available if the plaintiff should prove his claim. In the former case by contrast the plaintiff is not entitled to any security.

2. *Ibid.*
3. [1980] 3 All E.R. 353.
4. [1982] 3 All E.R. 36.
5. [1983] 2 All E.R. 158. For a more recent example see *The Mercantile Group (Europe) AG* v. *Aiyella*, unreported 27 November, 1984 (Lexis transcript).
6. [1983] 2 All E.R. 158 at p. 202.

He added that such a trust could only exist in respect of a defined asset or fund, and that even where a prima facie case had been made out for a trust fund, the wording of the order was still a matter for the discretion of the court, so that withdrawals for living expenses and legal costs could still be provided.

6. Costs

In *Faith Panton Property Plan Ltd.* v. *Hodgetts*[7] a Mareva injunction was granted to protect a judgment for costs which, at the time, had not been taxed. The case, described by Waller, L.J. as being of an "intermediate nature", raised problems as there was no question of the plaintiff being "likely" to obtain judgment; that had already been obtained, but the judgment would remain unenforceable for some months until taxation had been completed. In these circumstances the Court of Appeal held that such a judgment could, under the pre-Mareva practice, be protected by the appointment of a receiver, and that as this practice rested on the same statutory power as that to grant a Mareva injunction, there was no reason why the court could not grant a Mareva injunction in the instant case.

7. Appeals

An appeal will lie from a first instance judgment whether the application is made *ex parte* or *inter partes*. The question for the appellate court to consider is whether the judge applied the correct legal principles. If it concludes that he did, it will not interfere with the exercise of discretion even though individual members of the appellate court would have made a different order if sitting at first instance.[8]

7. [1981] 2 All E.R. 877.
8. *The Neidersachsen* [1983] 2 Lloyd's Rep. 600, [1984] 1 All E.R. 398; *Buchmann* v. *Hayden*, unreported 28 Sept. 1983 (Lexis transcript); *Henry Boot Building Ltd.* v. *The Croydon Hotel and Leisure Company Ltd.*, unreported 25 January, 1985 (Lexis transcript).

8. Ancillary Orders

Within a few years of the Mareva injunction being established it became clear that its value would be seriously diminished if the defendant deliberately concealed his assets or was evasive as to their whereabouts. This problem could, in part, be overcome by making an order against the total assets of the defendant within the jurisdiction, albeit, concealment of the existence of such assets would make it impossible for the plaintiff to "police" the injunction, and against a defendant determined, at all costs, to remove his assets from the plaintiff's clutches, it did not offer a practical solution. Further, where assets of the defendant were in the hands of third parties, especially banks, and the third party was the only one who could supply the necessary details of the value, nature and location of the assets, neither a total asset order, nor any other accepted form of order, would enable the plaintiff to reap the full benefits of the remedy.

The courts were swift to react. In most of the early "trust fund"[9] cases the courts granted orders ancillary to the injunction, such as for discovery or the administration of interrogatories to ensure that the Mareva jurisdiction" . . . is properly exercised and thereby to secure its objectives which is . . . the prevention of abuse.[10] The power to make ancillary orders for this purpose was confirmed by the Court of Appeal in *A. J. Bekhor & Co.* v. *Bilton*[11] where Griffiths, L.J. pointed out:

If the court has power to make a Mareva injunction it must have power to make an effective Mareva injunction. If the injunction will not be effective it ought not to be made.[12]

9. See the cases cited at pp. 56–58 *supra*.
10. *Per* Robert Goff, J. in *A.* v. *C.* [1980] 2 All E.R. 347 at p. 351.
11. [1981] Q.B. 293, [1981] 2 All E.R. 565, [1981] 2 Lloyd's Rep. 491.
12. *Ibid.* at p. 582.

9. Jurisdiction to make ancillary orders

The jurisdiction to make such necessary ancillary orders is derived from the same source as the jurisdiction to order a Mareva injunction, namely s.37 of the Supreme Court Act 1981, formerly s.45 of the Supreme Court of Judicature (Consolidation) Act 1925. As Ackner, L.J. remarked in *A. F. Beckhor & Co.* v. *Bilton*:[13]

> . . . It is now clearly established that the power of the High Court under s.45(1) includes the power to grant an interlocutory injunction to restrain a party to any proceedings from removing from the jurisdiction where that party is, as well as where he is not, domiciled, resident or present within that jurisdiction. . . . To my mind there must be inherent in that power, the power to make all such ancillary orders as appear to the court to be just and convenient, to ensure that the exercise of the Mareva injunction is effective to achieve its purpose.

Alternatively, the court has an inherent power to make such orders where they are reasonably necessary for the enforcement of an injunction to some similar order. Although this explanation was preferred by Stephenson, L.J. in the *Bilton* case,[14] and although such jurisdiction undoubtedly exists, a general acceptance in later cases of the power arising under statute[15] renders further consideration of it unnecessary.

The power to make such ancillary orders however, does not extend to enable the court to "police" the injunction, but may only be used where it is just and convenient in the enforcement of the injunction itself. Restraint, therefore, is necessary in the making of such an order. This restriction is

13. [1981] 2 All E.R. at p. 576.
14. [1981] 2 All E.R. at pp. 585–6.
15. *The Mercantile Group (Europe) AG* v. *Aiyella*, unreported 27 November, 1984 (Lexis transcript); *House of Spring Gardens Ltd.* v. *Waite*, unreported 1984, The Times 12 November, The Financial Times 13 November (Lexis transcript). *Cf.* the comments of Lawton, L.J. in *CBS (UK) Ltd.* v. *Lambert* [1982] 3 All E.R. 237.

well illustrated by *A. J. Bekhor & Co.* v. *Bilton.* A Mareva injunction there prohibited the defendant from removing assets in excess of £250,000 from the jurisdiction, albeit the terms were later varied to permit the defendant to remove certain living expenses and pay certain legal costs. The plaintiffs later adduced evidence that the defendant had not complied with the terms of the injunction and that his disclosures in his affidavits were not truthful. The plaintiffs therefore sought an order for discovery and for the administration of interrogatories. The application, granted at first instance, was refused by Ackner and Stephenson, L.J. on the ground that such an order would go further than was necessary to enforce the injunction, as the necessary information could be elicited by cross-examining the defendant on his affidavit. Griffiths, L.J. dissented, feeling that as the effect of such an order would be to enforce the injunction, it should be made notwithstanding that alternative methods were available, provided it did not offend the necessity of restraint.

10. Orders made under the power

(i) *Discovery*

The court may make an order for discovery against the defendant[16] or against a third party[17] to the extent that it is necessary to enforce the injunction.[18] Where the defendant's affidavit submitted under this order is unsatisfactory, the court may order a further affidavit to be submitted.[19] An application for an order for discovery may be made at

16. *A. J. Bekhor & Co.* v. *Bilton* [1981] Q.B. 293, [1981] 2 All E.R. 565, [1981] 2 Lloyd's Rep. 491.
17. *London and Counties Securities Ltd.* v. *Caplan,* unreported 1978; *Meditterania Raffinaria Sicilliana Petroli Spa* v. *Marbanaft GmbH,* unreported 1978; *A.* v. *C.* [1980] 2 All E.R. 347. *Bankers Trust Co.* v. *Shapira* [1980] 3 All E.R. 353.
18. *Cf. A. J. Bekhor & Co.* v. *Bilton* [1981] Q.B. 293, [1981] 2 All E.R. 565, [1981] 2 Lloyd's Rep. 491.
19. *Cf. House of Spring Gardens Ltd.* v. *Waite,* unreported 1984.

the time of the original application for the injunction or in a later application.[20]

(ii) *Interrogatories*

The court may make an order for the administration of interrogatories against the defendant in the same circumstances as it may make an order for discovery.[21] The fact that the answers will be likely to incriminate the defendant, particularly by showing non-compliance with the injunction, is no bar to such an order.[22]

(iii) *Cross-examination on the affidavit*

The court may order the defendant to be cross-examined on his affidavit either before or at the trial.[23]

(iv) *Oral examination of the defendant*

In cases where discovery may be ordered the court also has power to order that such discovery be made by oral examination of the defendant rather than by affidavit where to do so appears to be the only just and convenient way of ensuring compliance with the injunction by ensuring that the relevant assets are identified before there is an opportunity to remove them from the jurisdiction.[24] Although the circumstances where such an order would be justified are probably rare, the power to make such an order undoubtedly exists. As Slade, L.J. pointed out in *House of Spring Gardens Ltd.* v. *Waite*:[25]

20. *PCW (Underwriting Agencies) Ltd.* v. *Dixon* [1983] 2 Lloyd's Rep. 197.
21. *A. J. Bekhor & Co.* v. *Bilton* [1981] Q.B. 293, [1981] 2 All E.R. 565, [1981] 2 Lloyd's Rep. 491.
22. *Ibid.* See also *House of Spring Gardens* v. *Waite*, unreported 1984.
23. *A. J. Bekhor & Co.* v. *Bilton* [1981] Q.B. 293, [1981] 2 All E.R. 565 [1981] 2 Lloyd's Rep. 491. See also R.S.C. Ord. 38 r.2.
24. *House of Spring Gardens Ltd.* v. *Waite*, unreported 1984.
25. *Ibid.* See also *Dayco Corp.* v. *Trachem Co. Ltd.*, unreported 27 November 1984 (Lexis transcript).

. . . it is by no means inconceivable that cases, albeit perhaps rare cases, could arise where the court could properly take the view (1) that the defendant in an action appeared determined both to put or keep his assets beyond the reach of the plaintiff, and to conceal the true nature and extent of these assets from the court; and (2) that, in the particular circumstances of the case, an immediate order for oral examination or cross-examination of the defendant was the only "just and convenient" way of ensuring that he would not deal with his assets so as to deprive the plaintiffs in the future of the fruits of any judgment. In such a case I consider it reasonably clear that s.37 would be wide enough to give the court the requisite power to make an immediate order obliging the defendant to give oral evidence, as "just and convenient" relief ancillary to the Mareva order.

The fact that the oral examination is not related to facts relevant to the trial of the action itself, is no bar to the making of such an order.[26]

The scope of such oral examination should be confined to firstly, ascertaining whether the defendant has complied with the obligations imposed under the order, insofar as such compliance is questioned and secondly, insofar as such obligations have not been complied with, to elicit the missing information which compliance would have provided.[27]

11. Order for investigation of assets

Where the extent and fullness of the defendant's disclosure is in dispute, the court may order that a firm of accountants be instructed to ascertain the identity and location of the assets, property and money of the defendant. The order may include assets held outside the jurisdiction, assets held jointly with other persons not parties to the action, and

26. *Ibid.*
27. *Ibid.*

assets either directly or indirectly under the defendant's control.[28]

12. Order for delivery up

The court may order that chattels of the defendant, especially those which may be easily realised, be delivered up for safe keeping to prevent their disposal.[29] Again, restraint must be exercised in making such an order, as the deprivation of chattels may, in some circumstances, have as injurious an effect on the defendant's business and his ability to earn his livelihood as the sudden termination of his liquidity.

In considering whether to make such an order, the following matters should be taken into account although it has been stressed that these are no more than guidelines, and should be observed in spirit, rather than by the letter.[30] *Prima facie*, such an order should only be made against chattels which, as far as can be shown by or inferred from the evidence, were acquired by the defendant as a result of the wrongdoing forming the plaintiff's substantive claim, although no rule of law or practice confines the courts' jurisdiction to such chattels. In any case, there must be clear evidence that the defendant is likely to dispose of the chattels or otherwise deal with them so as to remove them from the court's jurisdiction unless he is restrained. Thus in *CBS (UK) Ltd.* v. *Lambert*[31] where the defendant was accused of "pirating" numbers of records and cassettes in which the plaintiffs held the copyright, and order for delivery up was made in respect of certain cars owned by the defendant, which were not used by him in any business,

---

28. See the order of the Court of Appeal in *PCW (Underwriting Agencies) Ltd.* v. *Dixon* [1983] 2 All E.R. 697.
29. R.S.C. Ord. 29 r. 2. See also *CBS (UK) Ltd.* v. *Lambert* [1982] 3 All E.R. 237.
30. *Ibid.*
31. [1982] 3 All E.R. 237.

which would be easily disposed of, and in view of the defendant's evasive conduct probably would be and which, in view of his allegation that he was, at all material times, unemployed, could only have been acquired by him with the proceeds of the "pirating" activities.

Secondly, no order should be made in respect of the defendant's wearing-apparel, bedding, tools of his trade, farm implements, livestock, machinery (including motor vehicles), materials, stock in trade or any other goods which the defendant is likely to use in the course of a lawful trade or business. Furnishings may be included in the above list, but where these constitute items of great value, such as *objets d'art.* and evidence shows that they were acquired for the purpose of frustrating execution, they may be included in an order for delivery up.

Thirdly, the order should clearly specify which chattels or classes of chattels are to be delivered up. If a plaintiff is unable to identify the chattels he wants delivered up, then *prima facie* no order should be made.

Fourthly, the order must not give the plaintiff a right to enter the defendant's premises for the purpose of seizing chattels covered by the order, and fifthly, delivery up should only be made to a receiver appointed by the Court, or to the plaintiff's solicitor where the court is satisfied that he can arrange safe and suitable custody for chattels delivered to him.

Sixthly, where chattels are in the possession, custody or control of third parties, the court should follow the guidelines applicable to the granting of injunctions over assets held by such third parties, insofar as they are applicable to chattels.[32]

Finally, provision should always be made for liberty to apply to stay, vary or discharge the order.

The nature of the ancillary orders differs little from analogous orders used in a substantive action. They are not

32. See the discussion at p. 78 *infra*.

of a peremptory nature, requiring instant obedience without the defendant having the opportunity to take legal advice as is the case with most Anton Piller orders.[33] Such orders may be conveniently used as an alternative to committal proceedings, and clearly, non-compliance with such an ancillary order will have the same consequences as non-compliance with the original order.[34]

33. See Chapter 7 *infra*.
34. *House of Spring Gardens* v. *Waite*, unreported 1984.

CHAPTER 5

EFFECT OF THE INJUNCTION

A Mareva injunction, like any other injunction, operates *in personam* against the defendant.[1] It operates from the time the order is made to prevent any disposal of assets covered by the order by the defendant, and extends to prevent third parties in possession or control of such assets from releasing them to the defendant's order in circumstances contrary to the terms of the injunction.[2] The effect was summed up by Lord Denning, M.R. in *Z. Ltd.* v. *A*[3]. in the following terms:[4]

> As soon as the judge makes his order for a Mareva injunction restraining the defendant from disposing of his assets, the order takes effect at the very moment that it is pronounced. ... Even though the order has not been drawn up, even though it has not been served on the defendant, it has immediate effect on every asset of the defendant covered by the injunction. Every person who has knowledge of it must do what he reasonably can to preserve the asset. He must not assist in any way in the disposal of it. Otherwise he is guilty of a contempt of court.

Every person whose actions could bring about a breach of the injunction is bound by its terms as soon as he has notice of them.[5] Although the order should normally be served on any party whom the order seeks to bind[6] informal notice

1. See the discussion in Chapter 1.
2. *Z. Ltd.* v. *A.* [1982] 1 All E.R. 556; *X County Council* v. *A*[1985] 1 All E.R. 53.
3. [1982] 1 All E.R. 556.
4. *Ibid.*, at p. 562.
5. *Carrow* v. *Ferrier* (1868) 17 L.T.(N.S.) 536. *Z. Ltd.* v. *A.* [1982] 1 All E.R. 556.
6. *Vansandau* v. *Rose* (1820) 2 J. & W. 264; *Gooch* v. *Marshall* (1860) 8 W.R. 410; *United Telephone Co.* v. *Duke* (1884) 25 Ch.D. 778.

will, where the urgency of the situation demands it, be sufficient. Thus, serving a notice, or giving notice by telephone will be sufficient.[7]

As the injunction does not amount to an arrest of the goods, (albeit it will have a similar effect if granted over specific goods) it does not prevent the defendant from discharging his obligations to others. In the case of a maximum sum order, or an order relating to specific assets, such discharge may be made by using other assets as the defendant is free to use his assets in the discharge of his obligations subject to the terms of the order. As Donaldson, L.J. pointed out in *Hitachi Shipbuilding and Engineering Co. Ltd.* v. *Viafiel Compania Naviera*:[8]

> There is no power in English law enabling a Court to order a defendant to provide security for a plaintiff's claims. All that can be done is to make an order which will prevent the defendant removing his assets from the jurisdiction or dissipating them within the jurisdiction and thus depriving the plaintiff of the fruits of any judgment or award which he may thereafter obtain. . . . Subject to this, any money or other assets of the defendant are freely available to him to use as he wishes in the running of this business and for ordinary daily living.

Where the defendant provides security for the plaintiff's claim, so as to secure the release of his assets from the injunction, the effect is to put the plaintiff in a stronger position, especially where the security is provided in the form of an undertaking by a third party, such as a bank guarantee, as the security will then be solely available to satisfy the plaintiff's claim, and cannot be claimed by other creditors of the defendant.[9]

In the case where the defendant's assets are covered *in*

7. *Cf. Gooch* v. *Marshall* (1860) 8 W.R. 410; *M'Neill* v. *Garratt* (1841) 10 L.J. Ch. 297, *Z. Ltd.* v. *A.* [1982] 1 All E.R. 556.
8. [1981] 2 Lloyd's Rep. 498 at pp. 508–9.
9. *Ibid.*

toto by the injunction, the defendant, or a third party claiming from the defendant, will need to seek the discharge or variation of the injunction before any payment or disposition is made by the defendant. Although the assets remain the unfettered property of the defendant, he may only dispose of them to the extent that the order, or variation of the order allows,[10] or the plaintiff consents.[11]

1. Debts and obligations which may be discharged subject to the variation or discharge of the injunction

(i) *Secured debts*

The holder of a security in respect of a debt from the defendant may seek to have the defendant's assets applied to the discharge of the debt.[12] In the case of a fixed charge, the variation would, presumably, permit the realisation of the subject matter of the security. In the case of a floating charge, a receiver must be appointed, thus crystallising the charge, before a variation may be properly made.[13]

Thus in *Cretanor Maritime Co. Ltd.* v. *Irish Marine Management Ltd.*[14] the owners of a vessel obtained judgment against the charterers in respect of a dispute which had been referred to arbitration. After the charterparty debt had been incurred, but before steps had been taken to enforce it, the charterers had created a floating charge secured by a debenture over all their assets. The owners obtained a Mareva injunction against the charterers before judgment was entered, but before judgment was executed a receiver was appointed under the debenture. The charterers' assets within the jurisdiction were insufficient to pay

10. *Ibid.* See also *Anglo Petroleum Ltd.* v. *Grant*, unreported 8 February, 1984 (Lexis transcript).
11. *Danae Shipping Corp. of Monrovia* v. *TPAO*, unreported 7 March, 1984 (Lexis transcript).
12. *Cretanor Maritime Co. Ltd.* v. *Irish Marine Management Ltd.* [1978] 3 All E.R. 164, [1979] 1 Lloyd's Rep. 491.
13. *Ibid.*
14. *Ibid.*

both the owners and the debenture holder, and an application was made to discharge the injunction so that the assets could be removed to satisfy the debenture holder's claim. This application was granted, the Court of Appeal pointing out that the holder of a Mareva injunction had no right to claim against the debtor's assets *in specie* and had to take his place in the normal queue of creditors. Buckley, L.J. pointed out:[15]

> The crystallisation of the floating charge does not. . . in any way conflict with the English injunction. . . In my judgment it is open to the debenture holder as equitable assignee. . . of the deposited fund in England to apply for the discharge of the injunction.

(ii) *Unsecured debts*

The position of an unsecured creditor is similar to that of a secured creditor, as the policy behind the Mareva injunction is to prevent the defendant from removing his assets so as to defeat the plaintiff's judgment, and not to prefer the plaintiff over other creditors.[16] This principle applies to allow a variation to enable the defendant to pay a debt which may not be strictly enforceable in law where it may be regarded as being payable in the normal course of business. Thus in *Iraqi Ministry of Defence* v. *Arcepey Shipping Co. (Gillespie Brothers and Co. Ltd. intervening), The Angel Bell*[17] a variation was permitted to allow the defendant's assets to be used to discharge a debt which was arguably illegal as being in breach of the Moneylenders Acts

---

15. *Ibid.*, at p. 172.
16. *Iraqi Ministry of Defence* v. *Arcepey Shipping Co. (Gillespie Brothers and Co. Ltd. intervening), The Angel Bell* [1980] 1 All E.R. 480; *Pharoas Plywood Co. Ltd.* v. *Allied Wood Products (PTC) Ltd.* unreported 1980. *Lloyd's Maritime Law Newsletter*; *A.* v.*B (X intervening)* [1983] 2 Lloyd's Rep. 532; *K/S A/S Admiral Shipping* v. *Portlink Ferries Ltd.* [1984] 2 Lloyd's Rep.
17. [1980] 1 All E.R. 480.

(since repealed). Robert Goff, J. was at pains to point out that the court, in permitting the variation, was not enforcing an illegal contract, but merely making it possible for the defendant to pay off what could be reasonably regarded as an ordinary business debt, and he pointed out:[18]

> The plaintiffs submit that I should not (permit the variation) for to do so might be to enforce an illegal transaction. I do not think that this is right. No doubt the court will not enforce, directly or indirectly, an illegal contract; but by lifting the Mareva injunction in the present case to enable the defendants to repay to the interveners the loan they have received would not be to enforce the transaction, even indirectly. A reputable businessman who has received a loan from another person is likely to regard it as dishonourable, if not dishonest, not to repay that loan even if the enforcement of the loan is technically illegal by virtue of the Moneylenders Acts. All the interveners are asking is that the defendants should be free to repay such a loan if they think fit to do so, not that the loan transaction should be enforced. For the defendant to be free to repay a loan in such circumstances is not inconsistent with the policy underlying the Mareva jurisdiction. He is not in such circumstances seeking to avoid his responsibilities to the plaintiff if the latter should ultimately obtain a judgment; on the contrary he is seeking, in good faith to make payments which he considers he should make in the ordinary course of business.

Similarly, a debt sounding in honour only, may be paid from assets otherwise subject to a Mareva injunction.[19] As Parker, J. pointed out in *A.* v. *B.* (*intervening*)[20] in relation to the intervener's claim based on certain dishonoured cheques drawn in his favour by the defendant:

Even, however, if the debt were unenforceable, it would not,

18. *Ibid.*, at p. 487.
19. *A.* v. *B.* (*X intervening*), [1983] 2 Lloyd's Rep. 532.
20. *Ibid.*

in my judgment matter, for a Mareva is not to be used to prevent a person meeting debts of honour, which this clearly was, so long as the court is satisfied that the defendant's desire to use assets caught by the injunction is not merely to evade its underlying purpose.

The above reasoning applies equally to domestic, as well as business debts, as Parker, J. pointed out, stating:[21]

> Equally, and for the same reason, the fact that the debt is not an ordinary business debt is of no importance. If a man has purchased for his own pleasure a valuable picture or a piece of furniture the injunction is not to be used to prevent him from paying the purchase price subject to the same qualification that the Court is satisfied that in doing so he is not evading its underlying purpose.

(iii) *Rights of set-off*

A creditor may claim the benefit of a right of set-off against a Mareva defendant even though in doing so the defendant's assets are reduced below the amount specified in a "maximum sum" order.[22] In *Oceana Castelana Armadora SA* v. *Mineralimportexport Ataka Navigation Inc., The Theotokos*[23] a Mareva injunction had been obtained against the assets of the Romanian Bank within the jurisdiction up to a maximum of \$2,190,060. Prior to the grant of the injunction, the Romanian Bank had deposited a sum with Barclays Bank International Ltd. to underwrite certain guarantees to be given by Barclays in respect of another matter. The guarantees were never issued. The holder of the injunction alleged that the money deposited with

---

21. *Ibid.*, at pp. 533–4.
22. *Oceana Castellana Armadora SA* v. *Mineralimportexport, The Theotokos* [1983] 2 Lloyd's Rep. 204; *Z. Ltd.* v. *A.* [1982] 1 All E.R. 556; *Project Development Co. Ltd. SA* v. *KMK Securities Ltd.* [1983] 1 All E.R. 465.
23. [1983] 2 Lloyd's Rep. 204.

Barclays was caught by the injunction, and could not be disposed of or dealt with by Barclays. Barclays had a number of term loans outstanding to the Romanian Bank and sought to set off interest which had accrued in respect of those loans both before and since the granting of the injunction against the fund belonging to the Romanian Bank. In holding that Barclays were so entitled Lloyd, J. pointed out:[24]

> It is now firmly established that a defendant who is subject to a Mareva injunction can apply to the Court to vary the injunction, so as to enable him to pay his ordinary debts as they fall due. If the defendant can thus, in a suitable case, draw on his bank account to pay his ordinary creditors, notwithstanding a Mareva injunction why should he not be free to pay his bank? Why should the bank be in a worse position than other ordinary creditors just because it is the bank which holds the funds in question?

In answer to the objection that the exercise of the right of set off would reduce the sum held below the "maximum sum" specified in the order he pointed out:[25] "But this is an inevitable consequence of a defendant who is subject to a 'maximum sum' . . . and who has no other free assets, being allowed to pay his debts as they fall due," and emphasised that the purpose of a Mareva was not to interfere with the lawful trade of third parties.

(iv) *Living expenses*

Provision for reasonable living expenses is usually made in the original order, where appropriate.[26] Where, however, the amount given is inappropriate to the defendant's lifestyle, it may be varied to take account of the defendant's

24. *Ibid.*, at p. 208.
25. *Ibid.*, at p. 209.
26. *A. J. Bekhor and Co. Ltd.* v. *Bilton* [1981] Q.B. 293, [1981] 2 All E.R. 565, [1981] 2 Lloyd's Rep. 491; *PCW (Underwriting Agencies) Ltd.* v. *Dixon* [1983] 2 All E.R. 158.

normal expenditure.[27] A defendant cannot be expected to drastically alter his lifestyle in the light only of an unproved claim, and the grant, especially on an *ex parte* application, of a wholly inadequate sum may be regarded as an attempt by the plaintiff to force the defendant to an early settlement.[28] Thus in *PCW (Underwriting Agencies) Ltd.* v. *Dixon*[29] the plaintiffs obtained a Mareva injunction on an *ex parte* application over the whole of the defendant's assets within the jurisdiction, on terms, *inter alia*, that the defendant be allowed £100 per week living expenses. At a subsequent *inter partes* hearing evidence was led that the defendant, a wealthy underwriter would, if confined to living on this sum, be forced to give up his residence at a London hotel, and to remove his sons from public school. In the circumstances, the amount was increased to £1,000 per week.

An allowance for living expenses may be made even where the plaintiff seeks a proprietary remedy by tracing on the "trust fund" basis.[30]

The power to vary for living expenses applies *mutatis mutandis* to provision to permit the party affected to carry on his day to day business.[31]

(v) *Legal and other costs*

Provision is frequently made in the original order to enable the defendant to defray his legal expenses in connection with the action, and the amount may be varied on subsequent application where it is reasonably necessary to do so.[32]

27. *PCW (Underwriting Agencies) Ltd.* v. *Dixon* [1983] 2 All E.R. 158.
28. *Ibid.*
29. *Ibid.*
30. *Ibid.*
31. *Purcell* v. *Geoprojects SARL*, unreported 21 July, 1983 (Lexis transcript).
32. *A. J. Bekhor and Co. Ltd.* v. *Bilton* [1981] Q.B. 293, [1981] 2 All E.R. 565, [1981] 2 Lloyd's Rep. 491; *PCW (Underwriting Agencies) Ltd.* v. *Dixon* [1983] 2 All E.R. 158 at first instance, and on appeal at [1983] 2 All E.R. 697; *A.* v. *C (No 2)* [1981] 2 All E.R. 126.

2. Application for variation

(i) *By the defendant*

No specific restraints are placed on a defendant in law when applying for a variation to enable him to discharge an obligation, but he must clearly show that this purpose in applying is not to defeat the policy underlying the Mareva injunction. As Sir John Donaldson, M.R. pointed out in *Campbell Mussels* v. *Thompson*,[33] having stated the basic principles behind the Mareva injunction:

> That is the principle; and if there is reason to believe that people are asking for money for school fees, doctors' bills, solicitors' costs or whatever, simply as a means of avoiding bringing free money into this country, or as a means of not having to use other moneys which have not been discovered and which they wish to keep out of the clutches of the court, of course, they will be refused. But the Mareva jurisdiction has never been intended to allow a plaintiff to put himself not only in the position of a secured creditor, but a secured creditor who is, on the basis of a contingent claim, entitled to priority over people who are dealing in the ordinary course of business with the defendant at that time.

Every case, therefore, must be judged on its own facts. It may be insufficient for the defendant to come to the court and say "I owe somebody some money" without disclosing whether he has other assets available from which the debt could be paid,[34] or to seek a variation where, on the evidence available, it is clear that the payment could not have been made had the injunction not been in force.[35]

(ii) *By third parties*

Before a variation or discharge may be ordered in favour of

33. Unreported 1984. The Times 30 May (Lexis transcript).
34. *A.* v. *C. (No. 2)* [1981] 2 All E.R. 126.
35. *A.* v. *B. (X Intervening)* [1983] 2 Lloyd's Rep. 532.

a third party it will usually be necessary for that party to intervene in the action upon which the Mareva injunction is based, albeit the court may, in drawing up the order, take account of the interests of third parties and reserve to them liberties to deal with the subject matter of the injunction.[36] Applications to intervene will usually be made under R.S.C. Ord. 15 r.6(2)(b)(ii)[37] which enables the court, on the motion of any party or on its own motion, to add as a party to the action:

> any person between whom and any party to the cause or matter there may exist a question or issue arising out of or relating to or connected with any relief or remedy claimed in the cause or matter which in the opinion of the Court it would be just and convenient to determine as between him and the party as well as between the parties to the cause or matter.

An application to be added under this rule, must usually show some interest in the subject matter over and above a commercial interest in the outcome of the action between the plaintiff and the defendant, but the extent of and limits to the applicant's duty have never been precisely defined. Kerr, L.J. in *Sanders Lead Co. Inc.* v. *Entores Metal Brokers Ltd.*[38] pointed out:

> In my view the rule requires some interest in the would-be intervener which is in some way directly related to the subject matter of the action. A mere commercial interest in its outcome, divorced from the subject matter of the action, is not enough. It may well be impossible, and would in any event be undesirable, to attempt to categorise the situations in which

36. See, for example, the order made in *Clipper Maritime Co. Ltd.* v. *Mineralimportexport, The Marie Lernhardt* [1981] 3 All E.R. 664, [1981] 2 Lloyd's Rep. 458, and note the comments of Lloyd, J. in *Oceana Castelana Armadora SA* v. *Mineralimportexport Atake Navigation Inc.*, *The Theotokos* [1983] 2 Lloyd's Rep. 204, at p. 209 col. 2.
37. For the equivalent power in Admiralty jurisdiction see R.S.C. Ord. 75 r. 17.
38. [1984] 1 All E.R. 857, at p. 863.

the interests of would-be interveners are sufficient to satisfy the requirements of the rule. The authorities show that the existence of a cause of action between the intervener and one of the parties is not a necessary prerequisite for this purpose. But they also go no further than to show that there must be some direct interest in the subject matter. . . .

Where the intervener claims he has a right of action he must show that he has an arguable case and that his case is not demurable.[39]

The power of the court to add parties under this rule is purely discretionary, and applications may be refused where there is an appropriate alternative means of protecting the intervener's interest,[40] or where the circumstances of the intervention suggest collusion or fraud.[41]

(a) **Application by creditors.** — A creditor of the defendant may clearly seek to intervene so as to have the injunction varied or discharged to permit his debt to be paid from the defendant's assets.[42] Where the creditor holds a debenture secured by a floating charge over the defendant's assets, the application should be made by the debenture holder himself, and not by a receiver appointed under the debenture where the receiver is, as will usually be the case, appointed as agent for the debtor.[43]

---

39. *Citibank NA* v. *Hobbs Saville and Co. Ltd. and Dray Shipping Co. Ltd. and A/S Seaheron*; *The Panglobal Friendship* [1978] 1 Lloyd's Rep. 368.
40. *Sanders Lead Co. Inc.* v. *Entores Metal Brokers Ltd.* [1984] 1 All E.R. 857.
41. *Fearman Ltd.* v. *The Dorset Corporation*, unreported 12 July, 1984 (Lexis transcript).
42. *Cretanor Maritime Co. Ltd.* v. *Irish Marine Management Ltd.* [1978] 3 All E.R. 164, [1979] Lloys's Rep. 491; *The Angel Bell* [1980] 1 All E.R. 480; *A* v. *B (X intervening)* [1983] 2 Lloyd's Rep. 532.
43. *Cretanor Maritime Co. Ltd.* v. *Irish Marine Management Ltd.* [1978] 3 All E.R. 164, [1979] 1 Lloyd's Rep. 491.

(b) Applications by banks. — A bank which holds a Mareva defendant's account is clearly prevented from making any payments in the normal course of business from the defendant's account to the extent to which the account is covered by the injunction other than payments which the bank cannot refuse to make, such as payments under guaranteed bills of exchange, letters of credit or cheques backed by a bankers' card.[44] Where the bank wishes to make other dispositions from the account it can apply for a variation, which will normally be granted in respect of payments made by the bank in the ordinary course of business and in the exercise of any right of set-off.[45] It has been urged that provision should be made in the original order to enable banks to discharge such obligations without having to apply to the court for an order for variation.[46]

(c) Third parties in possession, custody or control of the defendant's assets. — Where the defendant's assets are in the possession, custody or control of a third party, that third party may apply to vary or discharge the injunction where it has the effect of immobilising his own assets or preventing him from using them in the course of his own business.[47] Thus, in *Galaxia Maritime SA* v. *Mineralimportexport, The Eleftherios*,[48] an injunction was obtained over a cargo of coal then loaded aboard the Eleftherios shortly before she was due to sail from Barry. The effect of the injunction was to prevent the vessel from sailing, to prevent the owner from fulfilling certain commercial obligations and to interfere with the crew's personal arrangements. The plaintiffs offered to indemnify the owner against any loss or damage suffered as a result of the

44. *Z. Ltd.* v. *A.* [1982] 1 All E.R. 556.
45. *The Theotokos* [1983] 2 Lloyd's Rep. 204.
46. *Ibid.*, *per* Lloyd, J. at p. 209, Col. 2.
47. *Galaxia Maritime SA* v. *Mineralimportexport, The Eleftherios* [1982] 1 All E.R. 796.
48. *Ibid.*

injunction. The owner nevertheless sought, and was granted, a discharge of the injunction, Eveleigh, L.J. remarking:[49]

> I regard it as absolutely intolerable that the fact that one person has a claim for a debt against another, that third parties should be inconvenienced in this way, not only to affect their freedom of trading but their freedom of action generally speaking.

The above reasoning should apply, *mutatis mutandis*, to the discharge of a Mareva injunction over a ship's bunkers where these are not owned by the shipowner.[50]

The applicant for a Mareva injunction may be required to accept, as a condition for the making of the order, that third parties in possession of the defendant's assets should be permitted to deal with them so as not to interfere with their own trading activities.[51]

3. Cost of third party applications

Where a third party is put to expense in complying with the terms of a Mareva injunction, he is clearly entitled to recover his reasonable costs of doing so from the plaintiff,[52] and may intervene to obtain an order for the payment of such costs.[53] The third party is restricted to recovering only those costs reasonably incurred in complying with the injunction. This is achieved by taxing the intervener's costs

49. *Ibid.*, at p. 799.
50. *Cf. Sanko Steamship Co. Ltd.* v. *DC Commodities (A'Asia) Pty Ltd.* [1980] W.A.R. 51; As to ownership of bunkers between shipowner and charterer, see *The Saint Anna* [1980] 1 Lloyd's Rep. 180. Also see *Stellar Chartering and Brokerage Inc.* v. *Efibanca–Ent Finanzlario Interbancario Spa, The Span Terza No. 2* [1984] I W.L.R. 27.
51. *Clipper Maritime Co. Ltd.* v. *Mineralimportexport, The Marie Lernhardt* [1981] 3 All E.R. 664, [1981] 2 Lloyd's Rep. 458.
52. *Z. Ltd.* v. *A.* [1982] 1 All E.R. 556.
53. *Project Development Co. Ltd. SA* v. *KMK Securities Ltd.* [1983] 1 All E.R. 465.

on a solicitor and own-client basis, with a special direction
that the party to whom such costs are awarded should bear
the burden of establishing that the costs claimed are
reasonable.[54]

4. The Mareva injunction and security for costs

In any action in the High Court the defendant may apply
for an order for security for costs where, *inter alia*, the
plaintiff is resident outside the jurisdiction. This rule
applies to a defendant to an action commenced by writ and
to a defendant to a counterclaim. The position of a plaintiff
who finds himself defending a counterclaim and who wishes
to apply for security for costs may find his application
refused if he has already obtained a Mareva injunction in
pursuance of his own action. In *Hitachi Shipbuilding and
Engineering Co. Ltd.* v. *Viafel Compania Naviera SA*[55] the
plaintiffs claimed a sum in excess of £17m from the
defendant for an alleged breach of a shipbuilding contract
and was granted a Mareva injunction over the defendant's
assets within the jurisdiction. The defendant counterclaimed £79m for an alleged breach of the same contract by
the plaintiff. The plaintiff applied for security for costs in
respect of the action on the counterclaim, adducing
evidence that the assets covered by the Mareva injunction
would not fully meet the claim, if successful, and therefore
not the costs. Rejecting the application the Court of Appeal
pointed out that an order for security for costs would not be
made against a foreign plaintiff who had substantial assets
within the jurisdiction which were permanently available to
satisfy an order for costs. The effect of the Mareva
injunction was to make such assets available to satisfy the
claim. It did not secure any claim, but put the holder in the
same position as if the other party were domiciled within

54. *Ibid.*
55. [1981] 2 Lloyd's Rep. 498.

the jurisdiction with assets permanently here. The possibility that the claim, if successful, would swallow up all the assets, leaving nothing for costs, did not alter the position The reasoning must now be read as to apply to a defendant domiciled or resident within the jurisdiction.[56]

56. See Chapter 2 *supra*.

CHAPTER 6

DISSOLUTION, BREACH AND ENFORCEMENT

DISSOLUTION

The injunction may be brought to an end and dissolved in a number of ways.

(i) *Provision of security by the defendant*

It is always open to the defendant to obtain the dissolution of the injunction and the release of his assets by putting up security to the value of the plaintiff's claim.[1]

(ii) *Withdrawal from action by the plaintiff*

If at any time during the interlocutory stage the plaintiff discontinues the action,[2] the injunction will be discharged, subject to the discretion of the court to impose such terms on either party as it thinks fit.[3] Thus, for example where it was alleged that the injunction was obtained by fraud, the court ordered the documents whereby the injunction was obtained to be retained in the court's custody.[4]

(iii) *Expiration of time*

Where the order is granted for a limited time it will expire at that time, unless an application is granted meanwhile to

1. *Third Chandris Shipping Corp.* v. *Unimarine SA, The Genie* [1979] 2 All E.R. 972, [1979] 2 Lloyd's Rep. 194; *Ninemia Maritime Corp.* v. *Trave Schiffarhrtsgessellschaft mbH and Co. KG*; *The Neidersachsen* [1984] 1 All E.R. 398, [1983] 2 Lloyd's Rep. 600.
2. R.S.C. Ord. 21 r.2.
3. *Reprobound Ltd.* v. *Central Bank of Nigeria*, unreported 8 November, 1983 (Lexis transcript).
4. *Ibid.*

extend it.[5] Thus, an order may be for a limited number of days,[6] until trial or further order[7] until judgment,[8] until a limited period after judgment[9] or until execution.[10] Although an interlocutory injunction would normally be discharged if the plaintiff entered judgment in default[11] the court has discretion to extend the injunction until execution.[12]

(iv) *Dismissal of action*

If the plaintiff's action is dismissed, any interlocutory injunction relating to that action will be discharged.[13]

(v) *Amortisation of assets*

Where the defendant's assets subject to the injunction are amortised as a result of dispositions permitted by the terms of the injunction or by a later variation of those terms, the effect on the injunction is not clear. There is no authority to support the proposition that the injunction is thereby discharged and as, where it is proposed to use the whole of the assets subject to the injunction to satisfy a pre-existing debt, an application must be made to discharge the injunction,[14] it may be presumed that such an application

5. *Ibid.*
6. See *e.g. ibid.*
7. See *e.g.*, *Purcell* v. *Geoprojects SARL*, unreported 21 July, 1983 (Lexis transcript); *Manufacture du Pontis* v. *Wake*, unreported 2 August 1984 (Lexis transcript).
8. *Mareva Compania Naviere SA* v. *International Bulkcarriers SA* [1975] 2 Lloyd's Rep. 509.
9. *Ibid.*
10. *Orwell Steel (Erection and Fabrication) Ltd.* v. *Ashphalt and Tarmac (U.K.) Ltd.* [1984] 1 W.L.R. 1097.
11. R.S.C. Ord. 13 r.6.
12. *Stewart Chartering Ltd.* v. *C. & O. Managements SA, The Venus Destiny.* [1980] 1 All E.R. 718.
13. *Green* v. *Pulsford* (1839) 2 Beav. 70.
14. *Cretanor Maritime Co. Ltd.* v. *Irish Marine Management Ltd.* [1978] 3 All E.R. 164, [1979] 1 Lloyd's Rep. 491.

would need to be made where the subject matter is amortised.

(vi) *Discharge on application of the defendant*

The right of the defendant to apply to have the injunction dissolved is being increasingly used.[15] The application, which must be made by motion or summons,[16] may be based on the failure of the plaintiff to satisfy the conditions for a grant[17] or, on appeal, on the ground of the misuse by the judge of his discretion.[18] The courts have been particularly vigilant, on hearing such applications, to discharge injunctions obtained by fraud or forgery,[19] or misrepresentation or non-disclosure of material facts,[20] and where the injunction was granted on an *ex parte* application these grounds will alone be sufficient for an order of discharge, the plaintiff then being debarred from maintaining the injunction on merits disclosed at the hearing of the application.[21] Where the injunction has been granted against two or more persons, each of them must seek an order for dissolution. A dissolution on the application of one defendant will not usually extend to the others.[22] Where, however, a Mareva injunction is granted against more than one defendant on an *ex parte* application, a subsequent order to dissolve the injunction on the appli-

15. *The Neidersachsen* [1984] 1 All E.R. 398, [1983] 2 Lloyd's Rep. 600.
16. *Regent Oil Co. Ltd.* v. *J. T. Leavsley (Inchfield) Ltd.* [1966] 2 All E.R. 454.
17. See Chapter 5 *supra*.
18. See Chapter 5 *supra*.
19. *Reprobound Ltd.* v. *Central Bank of Nigeria*, unreported 8 November, 1983.
20. *Negocios Del Mar SA* v. *Doric Shipping Corp. SA, The Assios* [1979] 1 Lloyd's Rep. 331; *Manufacture du Pontis* v. *Wake, supra. Dynawest International Ltd.* v. *Margate Resources Ltd.*, unreported 9 November, 1984 (Lexis transcript).
21. *A-G* v. *Corporation of Liverpool* (1835) I.M. & C. 171; *Dalgleish* v. *Jarvie* (1850) 2 Mac & G 231.
22. *Bramwell* v. *Halcomb* (1836) 3 M. & C. 737.

cation of one defendant may be extended to discharge the order against the other defendants even though they take no part in the proceedings.[23] Where the court dissolves the injunction, an enquiry as to damages will usually be ordered where the plaintiff has not been guilty of misrepresentation or other default in obtaining it.[24]

(vii) *Dissolution on the application of a third party*

A third party who is directly affected by the terms of the injunction may apply for it to be dissolved.[25] Thus, a creditor of the defendant may apply for a dissolution so as to release the defendant's assets for the payment of his debt, and to release assets constituting security for his debt.[26] Parties in possession of the defendant's assets subject to the injunction, such as banks[27] or bailees of the assets,[28] may also apply.

Form of dissolution

In most cases the dissolution will be absolute. The court, however, has discretion to partially discharge the injunction, leaving some of the original assets covered by it still subject to the order,[29] or to dissolve it subject to a condition to be fulfilled by the defendant, such as the payment of a specified sum into court.[30]

---

23. *R. D. Harbottle (Mercantile) Ltd.* v. *National Westminster Bank Ltd.* [1978] Q.B. 146, [1977] 2 All E.R. 862.
24. *Griffiths* v. *Blake* (1884) 27 Ch.D. 474. For the effect of misrepresentation or non-disclosure on an *ex parte* application see *Ross* v. *Buxton* [1888] W.N. 1024.
25. *Bourbard* v. *Bourbard* (1864) 12 W.R. 1024.
26. *Cretanor Maritime Co. Ltd.* v. *Irish Marine Management Ltd.* [1978] 3 All E.R. 164, [1979] 1 Lloyd's Rep. 491.
27. *Z. Ltd.* v. *A.* [1982] 1 All E.R. 556.
28. *Galaxia Maritime SA* v. *Mineralimportexport* [1982] 1 All E.R. 796.
29. *Reprobound Ltd.* v. *Central Bank of Nigeria,* unreported 8 November, 1983.
30. *Purcell* v. *Geoprojects SARL,* unreported 21 July, 1983.

BREACH

The terms of a Mareva injunction, in common with the terms of any injunction, must be obeyed to the letter,[31] and a breach of such terms by anyone having notice of them will amount to a contempt of court,[32] except in cases of ambiguity on the face of the order[33] or emergency rendering compliance impossible.[34] Thus, where a defendant having full knowledge of the terms of a Mareva injunction acts in breach of its terms he will be guilty of contempt.[35] Where a third party to whom a Mareva injunction applies by virtue of his being in possession or control of assets of the defendant subject to the injunction, having full knowledge of the terms of the injunction acts in breach of these terms he may, according to the circumstances, be guilty of contempt and/or of aiding and abetting a contempt by the defendant.[36] A third party, however, will not be guilty of contempt unless the defendant himself has notice of the injunction.[37]

It is essential that the party who transgresses the terms of a Mareva injunction has knowledge of what he is doing; there is no longer any requirement that he should commit the breach "wilfully".[38]

Where a Mareva injunction affects property of, or held by, a company, the company may be guilty of contempt if a breach is knowingly committed by the person in control of the company, in circumstances where that person may be

---

31. *Hunt* v. *Hunt* (1894) 54 L.J.Ch. 289.
32. *Eastern Trust Co.* v. *McKenzie Mann & Co. Lim.* [1915] A.C. 750.
33. *Spokes* v. *Banbury Board of Health* (1865) L.R. 1 Eq. 42.
34. *Adair* v. *Young* (1879) 12 Ch.D.13.
35. *A. J. Bekhor & Co. Ltd.* v. *Bilton* [1981] Q.B. 293, [1981] 2 All E.R. 565, [1981] 2 Lloyd's Rep 491.
36. *Z. Ltd.* v. *A.* [1982] 1 All E.R. 556.
37. *Ibid.*
38. *Cf.* R.S.C. Ord. 45 r. 5. *Heatons Transport (St. Helens) Ltd.* v. *Transport and General Workers Union* [1972] 3 All E.R. 101; *Z Ltd.* v. *A.* [1982] 1 All E.R. 556.

regarded as the company's alter ego.[39] Where the act constituting the breach is committed by a servant of the company who knowingly assists in the breach of the terms of the injunction whilst acting in the course of his employment, the company will be regarded as guilty of contempt, whether civil or criminal,[40] on the ground of vicarious liability.[41] Again, knowledge of the breach is an essential element, the same test being applied as for an employer's liability for fraudulent misrepresentation in respect of the acts of his employees.[42] Thus, where a bank honours a cheque against a defendant when a Mareva injunction applies against his assets, it will be necessary in proving contempt, to show that the bank took reasonable steps to give notice to its employees of the restriction on that account, and the reasonableness of the bank's action may only be judged in the light of all the circumstances of the case.[43] Eveleigh L.J. in *Z. Ltd.* v. *A.* pointed out:[44]

I . . . do not think that the fact that one of the bank's officials is given notice of the terms of an injunction obliges the bank to undertake searches, in order to discover whether or not at any of its branches the bank holds the defendant's account. On the other hand, it will obviously be prudent, and in its own interests, for the bank to take some steps in the matter. If it does nothing, and a cheque is cashed or some other transaction completed, the bank may find it difficult to resist an inference that there was complicity in or connivance at the breach. It will be a question of fact and degree in every case. The greater the difficulty in discovering the account and consequently controlling it, the less likely the risk of contempt of court.

39. *Lennard Carrying Co.* v. *Asiatic Petroleum* [1915] A.C. 705. *The Lady Gwendoline* [1965] P. 294.
40. *Scott* v. *Scott* [1913] A.C. 417.
41. *Z. Ltd.* v. *A.* [1982] 1 All. E.R. 556.
42. *Ibid.* See also *Anglo-Scottish Beet Sugar Corp.* v. *Spalding U.D.C.* [1937] 2 K.B. 607. *Armstrong* v. *Strain.* [1952] 1 K.B. 139.
43. *Z. Ltd.* v. *A.* [1982] 1 All E.R. 556.
44. *Ibid* at p. 570.

The requirement to prove that the bank acted knowingly is particularly important for the protection of banks in the case of maximum sum orders, as those in control of the bank cannot be expected to know the identity of every account at every branch, and to find out such information would involve the bank in complicated and expensive administrative proceedings. Hence the importance of specifying the accounts subject to a maximum sum order, as in the absence of such specification it will rarely, if ever, be possible to show that a bank is in contempt.[45]

Where an injunction is granted against an individual, and acts constituting a breach are committed by a company of which he is a director, there will be no contempt on the part of the individual unless complicity in the breach can be shown.[46]

ENFORCEMENT

A Mareva injunction may be enforced either through ancillary orders[47] or through the traditional methods of punishing both civil and criminal contempt, namely by sequestration or committal, both of which have been used in relation to Mareva injunctions.[48]

Sequestration

A Mareva injunction being an '. . . order requiring (the defendant) to abstain from doing an act', the court has power on the application of the plaintiff to order sequest-

45. *Ibid.*
46. *Cf. Seaward* v. *Paterson* [1897] 1 Ch. 545.
47. See Chapter 4 *infra.*
48. *Anglo Petroleum Ltd.* v. *Grant*, unreported 8 February, 1984 (Lexis transcript). *Coutts & Co.* v. *Leonard*, unreported 6 April, 1984 (Lexis transcript). *Hill Samuel & Co. Ltd.* v. *Littaur*, unreported 21 December 1984 (Lexis transcript).

ration of the defendant's property in the case of a breach[49] or, where the defendant is a corporation, order sequestration against the director or any other officer of that body.[50]

Committal

Likewise the court may commit a defendant who is in breach of a Mareva injunction,[51] a power which extends to any person aiding or abetting the breach of such an injunction.[52] This power may be exercised against a defendant who is in breach of an order made ancillary to a Mareva injunction.[53]

The purposes of making an order for committal are twofold. As Bigham, J. pointed out in *Hill Samuel & Co. Ltd. v. Littaur*[54]

> I bear in mind that in making an order for committal, the Court has two purposes in view: one, that of punishing disobedience to an order of the court, and secondly, in the ordinary case, of coercion designed to induce obedience to the order.

Evidence that imprisonment will not induce obedience will not curtail the court's powers or limit its discretion,[55] but such evidence has led the court to order the release of the defendant before the sentence has been served in full.[56]

It must be borne in mind in applying for an order for committal that:

49. *A. J. Bekhor & Co. Ltd.* v. *Bilton* [1981] 2 All E.R. 565.
50. R.S.C. Ord. 45 r.5(1)(ii).
51. *Ibid.*, r.5(1)(iii).
52. *Hubbard* v. *Woodfield* (1913) 57 S.J. 729. *Z. Ltd.* v. *A.* [1982] 1 All E.R. 556.
53. *A. J. Bekhor & Co. Ltd.* v. *Bilton* [1981] Q.B. 293, [1981] 2 All E.R. 565, [1981] 2 Lloyd's Rep. 491.
54. Unreported 21 December, 1984.
55. *Ibid.*
56. *Enfield London Borough Council* v. *Mahoney* [1983] 2 All E.R. 901.

. . . the court does not contemplate any such step unless there is a clear and unambiguous order of which the alleged offenders are unequivocally in breach and, moreover, it must be shown that the order with which they have failed to comply is one which has been brought to the attention of the individuals concerned.[57]

As regards notice, the defendant should be served with a copy of the order[58] (or, where the defendant is a body corporate, the officer whom it is sought to commit must be so served[59]) and this copy should be endorsed with a "penal" notice stating the consequences of failing to obey the order.[60] To this rule there are five exceptions. First, service of an order for discovery and production of documents;[61] secondly, service of an order to answer interrogatories.[62] Thirdly, the court may order committal where it is satisfied that, pending service of the copy, the defendant in fact had notice of the order either through being present in court when the order was made or by being notified of the terms of the order by telephone, telegram or otherwise.[63] This exception only applies where the applicant has subsequently served or attempted to serve a copy of the order and does not enable service to be dispensed with.[64] The terms of the order referred to are the order in respect of which breach is alleged, and consequently where several orders have been made against the defendant the court must be satisfied that the terms of the correct order were brought to the defendant's attention.[65] Fourthly, where substituted service

57. *Per* Leggart, J. in *Coutts & Co.* v. *Leonard*, unreported 6 April, 1984.
58. R.S.C. Ord. 45 r.7(2)(a).
59. *Ibid* r.7(3)(a).
60. *Ibid.*, r.7(4). *Anglo Petroleum Ltd.* v. *Grant*, unreported 8 February, 1984.
61. *Ibid.*, r.7(2) and Ord. 24 r.16(3).
62. *Ibid.*, r.7(2) and Ord. 26 r.6(3).
63. *Ibid.* r.7(6).
64. *Hill Samuel & Co. Ltd.* v. *Littaur*, unreported 21 December, 1984.
65. *Ibid.*

is ordered,[66] and fifthly, where the court thinks it just to dispense with service of the copy of the order.[67] This last exception gives the court an unfettered discretion in respect of both mandatory and prohibitive orders,[68] and may be of particular use where the defendant has sought to evade service.[69]

In showing that a defendant has acted in breach of an order with knowledge of its terms, the quasi-criminal nature of committal must be considered, and the burden of proof will be that appropriate to criminal cases.[70]

In the case of civil contempt a maximum term of imprisonment of two years may be imposed,[71] and the court has power to suspend any sentence it imposes.[72]

66. R.S.C. Ord. 45 r.7(7) and Ord. 65 r.4.
67. *Ibid.*
68. *Hill Samuel & Co. Ltd.* v. *Littaur*, unreported 21 December, 1984.
69. *Ibid.*
70. *Ibid.* See also *Anglo Petroleum Ltd.* v. *Grant*, unreported February 8, 1984.
71. Contempt of Court Act 1981, s.14.
72. R.S.C. Ord. 52 r.7.

CHAPTER 7

ASSOCIATED ORDERS

Two other orders within the jurisdiction of the High Court restrain the defendant in the free use of his property before trial or execution, as the case may be. The first of these to be considered, the Anton Piller order, developed almost contemporaneously with the Mareva injunction, and both types of order are frequently sought in support of the same action. A brief summary of the right of arrest in Admiralty jurisdiction is also considered in this chapter.

ANTON PILLER ORDERS

At about the same time as the Mareva injunction was being developed to protect the potential fruits of the plaintiff's judgment, another procedural device in the form of an interlocutory injunction emerged to protect and preserve certain items of evidence vital to the plaintiff's case from destruction by the defendant. The early application of this type of order involved the preservation of "pirated" records, films, audio tapes and video tapes in actions brought in respect of breach of copyright in such items. Such breaches usually took the form of copies being made of a record or film without the consent of the owner of the copyright, and sold for a very low price in numerous back street shops and similar outlets, at great cost, in lost royalties, to the owners of the copyright. Despite the clear breach of copyright, the bringing of a successful action by the offended owners was complicated by the fact that as soon as a seller of the illegal wares caught wind of any impending action he would dispose of his stock before the plaintiffs could enforce discovery, and subsequently swear that he had only one or two illegal copies in his possession and that he could not remember where he obtained them.

If a plaintiff were to succeed in such an action, therefore, he needed to have access to the incriminating material before the "pirate", or illegal seller, could dispose of it. To meet this need, an order granted on an *ex parte* application and now known as the Anton Piller order, was made at first instance in 1974[1] and the right of the court to thus act was confirmed two years later by the Court of Appeal in *Anton Piller K.G.* v. *Manufacturing Processes Ltd.*,[2] from which the order takes its name. The basic form of order, (which has been modified since, when necessary to take account of the circumstances of the case)[3] required the defendant to permit the plaintiff and/or his authorised representative (usually his solicitor) to enter the defendant's premises and seize or take copies of relevant documents or goods, and to answer any interrogatories specified in the order.

It was at first contemplated that such order would be rare and would be made only in exceptional circumstances, and that plaintiffs would seek it only with caution.[4] Subsequent practice has shown not only a wide use of the remedy, but sometimes too free a use, without proper precautions being taken by the plaintiff to see that the application is justified.[5]

The application of the order was soon extended beyond "pirating" actions in relation to films and records, and was

1. *EMI Records Inc.* v. *Aram Darakdjian*, 21 May *EMI Ltd.* v. *Khazan*, 3 July; *Pall Centre Ltd.* v. *Microfiltrex Ltd.* 28 October. The first reported case was *EMI* v. *Pandit* [1975] 1 All E.R. 418, in which reference was made to the above cases at p. 423.
2. [1976] 1 All E.R. 779. The House of Lords confirmed the jurisdiction in *Rank Film Distributors Ltd.* v. *Video Information Centre* [1982] A.C. 380, but the point was not there in issue.
3. For a discussion of the form and extent of such orders see p. 104 *et seq.*
4. See the remarks of Templeman, J. in *EMI Records Ltd.* v. *Pandit* [1975] 1 All E.R. 418 at p. 424, and the judgments of Lord Denning, M.R. and Ormerod, L.J. in *Anton Piller K.G.* v. *Manufacturing Processes Ltd.* [1976] 1 All E.R. 779.
5. See, in particular, the remarks of Whitford, L.J. in *Systematica Ltd.* v. *London Computer Centre Ltd.* [1983] F.S.R. 313.

extended to other aspects of intellectual property,[6] to matrimonial disputes[7] and to commercial cases.[8] The order is widely used in the Commercial Court and is often sought as a means of enforcing a Mareva injunction.[9]

Such an order, albeit backed up by an undertaking in damages by the plaintiff may, for all the restraints placed upon its execution, be devastating to the defendant both commercially and personally, and the courts have emphasised the need for care and caution against abuse. As Woolf, J. remarked in *H.P.S.I.* v. *Thomas*.[10]

> The facts of the matter . . . make it clear that the concern which has been voiced by the courts from time to time as to the Draconian effect of such an order is fully justified and, if nothing else, they illustrate the care which should be exercised before such orders are made and above all, the discretion which should be exercised by those responsible for executing the orders.

Although Anton Piller orders have been fully accepted by the courts of this country an appeal against the right of courts to impose such restrictions on a defendant is currently before the European Commission of Human Rights.[11]

The jurisdiction to make Anton Piller orders has been

---

6. See, for example, *Universal City Studios Inc.* v. *Mukhtar & Sons Ltd.* [1976] 1 W.L.R. 568 — trade mark in T-shirt design; and *Anton Piller K.G.* v. *Manufacturing Processes Ltd.* [1976] 1 All E.R. 779 — computer hardware design.
7. *Emmanuel* v. *Emmanuel* [1982] 2 All E.R. 342.
8. *PCW (Underwriting Agencies) Ltd.* v. *Dixon* [1983] 2 All E.R. 697.
9. For a recent example see *Distributori Automatici Italia Spa* v. *Holford General Trading Co. Ltd.*, unreported 9 November, 1984 (Lexis transcript).
10. (1983) 133 N.L.J. 598 (Lexis transcript).
11. An application for release of documents seized under an Anton Piller order to enable such an application to be pursued, was made in *ITC Film Distributors Ltd.* v. *Video Exchange Ltd.*, unreported 10 February, 1983 (Lexis transcript).

accepted in many common law countries,[12] albeit in New Zealand,[13] South Africa,[14] Malaysia,[15] and Hong Kong[16] the courts have been at pains to emphasise the exceptional nature of the remedy, and to echo the earlier judgments of English courts that its use should be rare and only in response to pressing need.

In civil law, the Anton Piller order has its equivalent in the French interlocutory remedy of *Saisie-contrefacon* under which similar rights may be exercised in respect of patents,[17] designs,[18] copyright[19] and trademarks.[20] Articles and documents may, under these provisions, be seized or, where appropriate, photographed.

1. Jurisdiction to make the order

R.S.C. Ord. 29 rr. 1 and 2 permit the court to order the detention, custody or preservation of any property which is the subject matter of any cause and may authorise any person to enter onto any land or building in the possession of any party to the cause or matter, on the application of any

12. See the remarks of Lord Frazer of Tullybelton in *Rank Film Distributors Ltd.* v. *Video Information Centre* [1982] A.C. 380 at pp. 444–5.
13. *Busby* v. *Thorn EMI Video Programmes Ltd.* [1984] 1 N.Z.L.R. 461.
14. *Romer Watch Co. SA* v. *African Textile Distributors* [1980] 2 S.A.L.R. 254, where the powers of seizure were specifically confined to powers which would normally be available on discovery. *Easyfind International (SA) (PTY) Ltd.* v. *Instaplan Holdings* [1983] 3 S.A.L.R. 917. See also *House of Jewels and Gems* v. *Gilbert* [1983] 4 S.A.L.R. 824 where the power to make such orders was confirmed as existing at common law and not under Roman-Dutch law.
15. *Television Broadcasts Ltd. Ors.* v. *Mandarin Video Holdings Sdn. Bdh.* [1983] 2 M.L.J. 409; *Lian Keow Sdn. Bdh.* v. *C. Paramjothy and Anor.* [1982] 1 M.L.J. 217.
16. *Technica Electronics Ltd.* v. *Shin-Shirasuna Denki Kabushiki Kaisha* [1981] H.K.L.R. 425.
17. Loi de Juilet 5, 1844, Arts. 47–48 *Journal du Palais* 2.29.
18. Loi de Juilet 14, 1909 J.O. Juilet 1, 1909.
19. Loi. No. 57–298 of March 11, 1957. J. O. March 11, 1957.
20. Loi No. 64–1360 of Dec. 31, 1964 J. O. Jan 1, 1965.

party to that cause or matter. An application for such an order must be made by summons or notice under Ord. 25 r. 7. This power was accepted as a sufficient basis to make an order of the Anton Piller type by Templeman, J. in *EMI Ltd.* v. *Pandit*[21] but was rejected by the Court of Appeal in *Anton Piller K.G.* v. *Manufacturing Processes Ltd.*[22] as being inapplicable to an *ex parte* application, and the power to make the order was held to rest on the inherent jurisdiction of the court. Lord Denning, M.R. pointed out[23]:

> So it falls to us to consider it on principle. It seems to me that such an order can be made by a judge *ex parte*, but it should only be made where it is essential that the plaintiff should have inspection so that justice can be done between the parties; and when, if the defendant were forewarned, there is a grave danger that vital evidence will be destroyed, that papers will be burnt or lost or hidden, or taken beyond the jurisdiction, and so the ends of justice be defeated; and when the inspection would do no real harm to the defendant or his case.

That being so[24] the jurisdiction may be exercised in circumstances not covered by Ord. 29, so as to enable the preservation of a document or item which is not itself the subject matter of the action.[25]

2. Nature of the order

An Anton Piller order is, in essence, a form of discovery, albeit a form of discovery for use in an emergency situation which is not covered by the Rules of the Supreme Court.[26]

21. [1975] 1 All E.R. 418.
22. [1976] 1 All E.R. 779.
23. *Ibid.*, at p. 783.
24. The principle was recently accepted and applied in *Distributori Automatici Italia Spa* v. *Holford General Trading Co. Ltd.*, unreported 9 November, 1984.
25. *Yousif* v. *Salama* [1980] 3 All E.R. 405.
26. *EMI Ltd.* v. *Pandit* [1975] 1 All E.R. 418. *Yousif* v. *Salama* [1980] 3 All E.R. 405.

It operates *in personam* against the defendant, provided he is within the jurisdiction.[27] As such, it is not equivalent to a search warrant in respect of the defendant's premises, and does not give the plaintiff or his representatives power to effect forcible entry.[28] It takes effect as a mandatory injunction against the defendant to allow the plaintiffs to enter, breach of which will put the defendant in contempt of court.[29]

As Templeman, J. put it in *EMI Ltd.* v. *Pandit*:[30]

An order in that form does not justify any unlawful entry. It imposes on the defendant a mandatory injunction ordering him to allow the plaintiffs to enter. It limits the persons who shall be allowed in to those whom counsel has satisfied me are necessary in the present case to inspect, identify and photograph infringing materials and other articles to which the plaintiffs are entitled. It does not order an entry on premises, unless they are in the occupation or use of the defendant, so that the rights of other persons who may be interested in the property are fully protected; and finally, it lays down reasonable hours for the exercise of the power which is granted by this order.

Although the effect of the order may appear limited, Lord Denning, M.R. pointed out in *Anton Piller K.G.* v. *Manufacturing Processes Ltd.*:[31]

One might think that with all these safeguards against abuse, it would be of little use to make such an order. But it can be effective in this way: it serves to tell the defendant that, on the

27. *Altertext Inc.* v. *Advanced Data Communications Ltd.* [1985] 1 All E.R. 395.
28. *EMI Ltd.* v. *Pandit* [1975] 1 All E.R. 418. *Anton Piller K.G.* v. *Manufacturing Processes Ltd.* [1976] 1 All E.R. 779; *Rank Film Distributors Ltd.* v. *Video Information Centre* [1982] A.C. 380.
29. *Altertext Inc.* v. *Advanced Data Communications Ltd.* [1985] 1 All E.R. 395. *Anton Piller K.G.* v. *Manufacturing Processes Ltd.* [1976] 1 All E.R. 779.
30. [1975] 1 All E.R. 418, at p. 424.
31. [1976] 1 All E.R. 779, at p. 783.

evidence put before it, the court is of the opinion that he ought to permit inspection, — nay, it orders him to permit — and that he refuses at his peril. It puts him in peril not only of proceedings for contempt, but also of adverse inferences being drawn against him; so much so that his own solicitor may often advise him to comply.

An order may only be sought in pursuance of an action already commenced, or which the plaintiff intends to commence in the very near future, and in the latter case especially, must only be used to preserve evidence in respect of that action. It is not to be used as part of a "fishing expedition" to enable the plaintiff to accumulate evidence in the light of which he may or may not decide to proceed, and he must issue his writ or pleadings within the statutory time.[32] The court may however, permit service out of time unless the delay is inordinate or inexcusable[33] but it must be borne in mind that, as the plaintiff has been given a special advantage and the defendant placed under restraint, the plaintiff is under a special obligation to proceed speedily.[34]

3. Conditions for the making of an order

Ormrod, L.J. in *Anton Piller K.G.* v. *Manufacturing Processes Ltd.* defined three essential pre-conditions for the making of an order, stating:[35]

> First, there must be an extremely strong *prima facie* case. Secondly, the damage, potential or actual, must be very serious for the plaintiff. Thirdly, there must be clear evidence that the

32. *Hytrac Conveyors Ltd.* v. *Conveyors International Ltd.* [1982] 3 All E.R. 415.
33. *Birkett* v. *James* [1977] 2 All E.R. 801. *M.K.O. (Nigeria) Ltd.* v. *Marcan Services (Export) Ltd.*, unreported 29 April, 1983 (Lexis transcript).
34. *Greek City Co. Ltd.* v. *Demetrion (Trading as Spectron Electronics)* [1983] 2 All E.R. 921.
35. [1976] 1 All E.R. 779, at p. 784.

defendants have in their possession incriminating documents or things, and that there is a real possibility that they may destroy such material before any application *inter partes* can be made.

Although these three conditions have been approved and applied subsequently,[36] other conditions have emerged in later cases.

(i) *The strength of the plaintiff's case*

This has been variously put, "strong *prima facie* case,[37] satisfactory evidence[38] and "strength of a case"[39] having been used to describe the plaintiff's duty. In essence, therefore, the plaintiff must lead evidence at the *ex parte* application which indicates that he has, at the time of the application, an arguable cause of action, and that the order is essentially in aid of the inquisitorial process of the action, and not necessary to enable the plaintiff to frame the action itself.[40] The plaintiff must convince the court, where necessary, that there is a valid juridical basis for his action.[41]

36. *Ex parte Island Records Ltd.* [1978] 3 All E.R. 824; *Rank Film Distributors Ltd.* v. *Video Information Centre* [1982] A.C. 380; *Randolph M. Fields* v. *Watts* (1984) 129 S.J. 67, The Times 22 November (Lexis transcript); *Jeffrey Rogers Knitwear Productions Ltd.* v. *Vinola (Knitwear) Manufacturing Co.* unreported 23 November, 1984 (Lexis transcript); *H.P.S.I.* v. *Thomas* (1983) 133 N.L.J. 598.
37. *Anton Piller K.G.* v. *Manufacturing Processes Ltd.* [1976] 1 All E.R. 779; *Vapormatic Co. Ltd.* v. *Sparex Ltd.* [1976] 1 W.L.R. 939.
38. *Universal City Studios Inc.* v. *Mukhtar & Sons Ltd.* [1976] 1 W.L.R. 568.
39. *Anton Piller K.G.* v. *Manufacturing Processes Ltd.* [1976] 1 All E.R. 779.
40. *Hytrac Conveyors Ltd.* v. *Conveyors International Ltd.* [1982] 3 All E.R. 415.
41. *Ex parte Island Records Ltd.* [1978] 3 All E.R. 824. The case concerned claims arising from the 'bootlegging' of records, *i.e.*, making illicit recordings of live performances and selling copies. As

(ii) *Actual or potential damage to the plaintiff*

This appears self explanatory at first sight, and has been applied, for example where, if certain of the documents in the defendant's possession were not released to the plaintiff, he would risk being in contempt of court in another jurisdiction.[42] It has been pointed out, however, that in applying the balance of convenience as in all interlocutory injunctions, account must be taken not only of the effect of not making the order on the plaintiff, but the effect of execution of the order on the defendant and that, especially where both parties are commercial concerns, an unacceptable level of damage may be done to the defendant by permitting the plaintiff access to premises where the plaintiff may see many items or documents otherwise confidential to the defendant's business which are not concerned with the action.[43]

(iii) *Real possibility of destruction or removal*

It would clearly be impossible for the plaintiff to prove that the relevant documents or items would be removed if litigation took its normal course, but evidence of the possibility must be adduced.[44] In considering the possibility the court will have particular regard to the character

to the legal position of bootlegging, see *Lonhro Ltd.* v. *Shell Petroleum Co. Ltd.* [1982] A.C. 173 as interpreted in *RCA Corp.* v. *Pollard* [1982] 3 All E.R. 771. See also *Lian Keow Sdn Bdh* v. *C. Paramjothy and Anor.* [1982] 1 M.L.J. 217 where an application before the High Court in Malaysia failed when the applicant was unable to prove legal ownership of the copyright which the defendant was alleged to have infringed.

42. *Randolph M. Fields* v. *Watts* (1984) 129 S.J. 67.
43. *Thermax Ltd.* v. *Schlott Industrial Glass Ltd.* [1981] F.S.R. 289; *Jeffrey Rogers Knitwear Productions Ltd.* v. *Vinola (Knitwear) Manufacturing Co.*, unreported 23 November, 1984.
44. *Universal City Studios Inc.* v. *Mukhtar & Sons Ltd.* [1976] 1 W.L.R. 568.

and status of the defendant[45] or, where the defendant is a company, to the character and standing of its directors.[46]

(iv) *Disclosure of material facts*

The applicant must disclose all facts material to the application, the importance of which has been emphasised in stating:[47]

> I think it is very important indeed that in making applications it should be in the forefront of everybody's mind that the court must be fully informed of all facts that are relevant to the weighing operation which the court has to make in deciding whether or not to grant the order.

This duty of disclosure involved:

> . . . not merely of disclosing those facts which may be inherently within the knowledge of the party making the application but the importance of applicants making, if necessary, such enquiries as ought reasonably to be made, touching matters which ought to be within the purview of the court.[48]

Failure to disclose all facts which should have been disclosed may result in the later discharge of the order.[49] The duty to disclose it is owed only to the court not to the defendant and a failure to make full disclosure will not render the plaintiff liable in damages.[50]

---

45. *Randolph M. Fields* v. *Watts* (1984) 129 S.J. 67.
46. *Thermax Ltd.* v. *Schlott Industrial Glass Ltd.* [1981] F.S.R. 289.
47. *Browne Elkinson, J.* in *Thermax Ltd.* v. *Schlott Industrial Glass Ltd.* [1981] F.S.R. 289 at p. 298.
48. *Per* Whitford J. in *Jeffrey Rogers Knitwear Productions Ltd.*, v. *Vinola (Knitwear) Manufacturing Co.*, unreported 23 November, 1984.
49. *Wardle Fabrics Ltd.* v. *G. Myristis Ltd.* [1984] F.S.R. 263.
50. *Digital Equipment Corp.* v. *Darkcrest Ltd.* [1984] 3 All E.R. 381.

(v) *Defendant within the jurisdiction*

An Anton Piller order will not be made on an *ex parte*
application against a defendant who is not within the
jurisdiction of the court unless the case is one where leave to
serve notice of the writ outside the jurisdiction would be
granted pursuant to R.S.C. Ord. 11, and even where an
Anton Piller order is granted the order should not be
executed until the defendant has had the opportunity to set
aside the leave given under Ord. 11, as until such time as
the court's assumption of jurisdiction can be regarded as
provisional only.[51] If the defendant can be properly served
within the jurisdiction the order, being *in personam*, may
apply to premises outside the jurisdiction.[52]

(vi) *Undertaking by the plaintiff*

As in any type of interlocutory injunction, the plaintiff
must give an undertaking to indemnify the defendant for
damage caused by compliance with the order if the plaintiff
should fail in his claim.[53] The adequacy of damages in this
respect may be a relevant consideration in deciding whether
to grant the order.[54] Where the plaintiffs are resident
outside the jurisdiction some form of security may be
required.[55] Although the Anton Piller cases have not dealt
with the point, and it seems unlikely to arise in practice, a
plaintiff should also indemnify a third party who suffers
loss or damage as a result of the enforcement of the order.[56]

51. *Altertext Inc.* v. *Advanced Data Communications Ltd.* [1985] 1 All
    E.R. 395.
52. *Cook Industries Inc.* v. *Galliher* [1978] 3 All E.R. 945.
53. *EMI Ltd.* v. *Pandit* [1975] 1 All E.R. 418; *Anton Piller K.G.* v.
    Manufacturing Processes Ltd. [1976] 1 All E.R. 779; *Vapormatic Co.
    Ltd.* v. *Sparex Ltd.* [1976] 1 W.L.R. 939; *W.E.A Records Ltd.* v.
    Visions Channel 4 Ltd. [1983] 2 All E.R. 589.
54. *Vapormatic Co. Ltd.* v. *Sparex Ltd.* [1976] 1 W.L.R. 939.
55. *Anton Piller K.G.* v. *Manufacturing Processes Ltd.* [1976] 1 All E.R.
    779.
56. *Cf. Z. Ltd.* v. *A.* [1982] 1 All E.R. 556.

4. The application

The application at first instance will be made *ex parte* and should be made by motion or summons.[57] As the application will usually be one of urgency the hearing may take place in chambers,[58] but where application is made in open court application should be made for a hearing in camera,[59] and the court may go into camera of its own motion, if no such application is made.[60] The application will usually be made before the writ is issued,[61] but the court has power to grant an order after judgment has been given in aid of execution.[62]

5. Service

Although the order must be served on the defendant before it can be enforced,[63] in view of the nature of the order and the need for peremptory obedience, the plaintiff, in serving the order should be accompanied by his solicitor.[64] It may be desirable that the solicitor, as an officer of the court, should effect the service.[65]

---

57. R.S.C. Ord. 29 r.1.
58. See *Practice Note* [1983] 1 All E.R. 1119.
59. *Anton Piller K.G.* v. *Manufacturing Processes Ltd.* [1976] 1 All E.R. 779; *Vapormatic Co. Ltd.* v. *Sparex Ltd.* [1976] 1 W.L.R. 939.
60. *Vapormatic Co. Ltd.* v. *Sparex Ltd.* [1976] 1 W.L.R. 939.
61. *Anton Piller K.G.* v. *Manufacturing Processes Ltd.* [1976] 1 All E.R. 779; *Rank Film Distributors Ltd.* v. *Video Information Centre* [1982] A.C. 380; *Yousif* v. *Salama* [1980] 3 All E.R. 405.
62. *Distributori Automatici Italia Spa* v. *Holford General Trading Co. Ltd.*, unreported 9 November, 1984.
63. See Chapter 5 *supra*.
64. *Anton Piller K.G.* v. *Manufacturing Processes Ltd.* [1976] 1 All E.R. 779.
65. *Vapormatic Co. Ltd.* v. *Sparex Ltd.* [1976] 1 W.L.R. 939.

6. Scope and Form of Order

An order may take a variety of forms and contain a number
of elements, according to the requirements of the case,
bearing in mind always what is sought to be achieved. The
precise limits of the courts' powers have never been
defined. The following elements have been included in
orders made to date.

(i) *Entry to premises*

The most basic part of any order is the requirement, in the
form of a mandatory injunction, that the defendant permit
the plaintiff and such persons as are specified in the order,[66]
to enter the premises named in the order, and there conduct
such searches as are deemed necessary. The plaintiff will be
given the right to remove or copy documents relevant to the
case,[67] (although the order may specify documents which
are not of immediate relevance to the substantive claim, if
they may materially effect the course of the action)[68], or to
remove goods relevant to the action.[69] The injunction may
also forbid the defendant from parting with, removing or
destroying documents or items in his possession.[70]

(ii) *Administration of interrogatories*

The order may permit the plaintiff to administer interroga-

---

66. For the importance of specifying such persons note the remarks of
    Graham, J. in *Vapormatic Co. Ltd.* v. *Sparex Ltd.* [1976] 1 W.L.R.
    939, at p. 940.
67. *Anton Piller K.G.* v. *Manufacturing Processes Ltd.* [1976] 1 All E.R.
    779; *Yousif* v. *Salama*, [1980] 3 All E.R. 405; *H.P.S.I.* v. *Thomas*
    (1983) 133 N.L.J. 598.
68. *Yousif* v. *Salama* [1980] 3 All E.R. 405.
69. *Universal City Studios Inc.* v. *Mukhtar & Sons Ltd.* [1976] 1 W.L.R.
    568; *Rank Film Distributors Ltd.* v. *Video Information Centre* [1982]
    A.C. 380; *Jeffrey Rogers Knitwear Productions Ltd.* v. *Vinola
    (Knitwear) Manufacturing Co.*, unreported 23 November, 1984.
70. *EMI Ltd.* v. *Pandit* [1985] 1 All E.R. 418.

tories to the defendant concerning such matters as the location of relevant information,[71] the source of his supply of goods,[72] or as to whether he has parted with possession of documents or other relevant information.[73] The order may further require the plaintiff to make disclosures, or verify the disclosures made in response to the interrogatories, by affidavit.[74]

(iii) *Confidentiality*

The order may require the defendant to keep all matters relating to the action in confidence, subject to such disclosures as will be necessary in the court of obtaining legal advice.[75]

(iv) *Right to consult solicitor*

The Anton Piller jurisdiction is, by its nature, peremptory, requiring immediate obedience without giving the defendant the opportunity to consult his solicitor, or to apply for a discharge.[76] In certain circumstances where the court thinks fit, however, especially where the order relates to the defendant's own home, the order may contain a provision enabling the defendant to consult a solicitor before complying with its remaining terms.[77]

(v) *Addressee*

An Anton Piller order operates *in personam* against the

71. *H.P.S.I.* v. *Thomas* (1983) 133 N.L.J. 598.
72. *Rank Film Distributors Inc.* v. *Video Information Centre* [1982] A.C. 308.
73. *H.P.S.I.* v. *Thomas* (1983) 133 N.L.J. 598.
74. *Ibid.*
75. *Ibid.*
76. *Altertext Inc.* v. *Advanced Data Communications Ltd.* [1985] 1 All E.R. 395, though *cf.* the remarks of Lord Denning M.R., in *Anton Piller K.G.*, v. *Manufacturing Processes Ltd.* [1976] 1 All E.R. 779, at p. 783.
77. *H.P.S.I.* v. *Thomas* (1983) 133 N.L.J. 598.

defendant, and thus will be addressed to him. It may, however, be extended to address such persons who are, or who appear to be, in charge of the premises.[78]

7. Ancillary Orders

The court has an inherent power to order that the defendant be cross-examined on his affidavit.[79] This power, however, will only be exercised where it is likely to enhance the enforcement of the order. As Peter Gibson, J. pointed out in *R.C.A. Corp.* v. *Allsop*[80]:

> . . . the court should not make an order for cross-examination unless satisfied that there was a reasonable likelihood that the person sought to be cross-examined had information which should have been disclosed pursuant to the order for disclosure and which would lead to the fulfilment of the purpose of such an order, that is to say, disclosure of sources and ascertaining the whereabouts of illicit goods.

In exercising this power, the court must avoid orders which are intended, or will have the effect of, showing contempt, or providing evidence for use at the trial, other than that contemplated by the Anton Piller order. Peter Gibson, J. also pointed out:[81]

> But in this area the court must proceed with caution. The object of the application must, I apprehend, truly be to obtain the further information which it is believed is in the possession of the person, the subject of the order, but that person has failed to disclose notwithstanding the earlier order. The object of the application must not be to enable contempt proceedings to be brought so as to punish the person served with the order.

78. *Ibid.*
79. *Bekhor & Co. Ltd.* v. *Bilton* [1981] Q.B. 293, [1981] 2 All E.R. 565, [1981] 2 Lloyd's Rep. 491; *R.C.A. Corp.* v. *A.J. Allsop*, unreported 3 October, 1984.
80. *Ibid.*
81. *Ibid.*

Further, it must be to obtain information which is to be used for the purpose of the action when that trial comes to action.

8. Rights over documents and property seized

Documents or property seized under an Anton Piller order may, subject to the terms of that order, be retained by the plaintiff's solicitors or other custodian appointed by the court against their undertaking to preserve them in safe custody.[82] Consequently, such custodians may not part with possession of the documents or reveal any part of their contents to any other party without the consent of the defendant or order of the court, or use them for any collateral or ulterior purpose of their own.[83] The undertaking given in this respect is the same as that given in a normal case of discovery, where the prohibition on such dealings is well established.[84]

Documents or goods seized as a result of an Anton Piller search which clearly have no bearing on the action, may on the application of the defendant be ordered to be returned to him unless the plaintiff returns them voluntarily.[85] Similarly, documents or goods so seized belonging to a third party may be ordered to be returned, but in considering an application for such a return, the court will take into account the strength of the third party's case in alleging ownership of the goods or documents, and whether justice would be best served by such an order.[86]

82. *Anton Piller K.G.* v. *Manufacturing Processes Ltd.* [1976] 1 All E.R. 779.
83. *Customs and Excise Commissioners* v. *A. E. Hamlin & Co.* [1983] 3 All E.R. 654.
84. *Ibid.* See also *Home Office* v. *Harman* [1982] 1 All E.R. 532.
85. *Randolph M. Fields* v. *Watts* [1984] 129 S.J. 67.
86. *Gramhill Ltd.* v. *A. E. Hamlin & Co.*, unreported 21 December, 1983 (Lexis transcript).

9. Breach of the order

A person on whom an Anton Piller order is served and who knowingly disobeys it, is guilty of contempt of court.[87] In view of the peremptory nature of the order this may appear harsh, but a defendant who refuses the plaintiff entry to his premises in the hope that a swift application will result in it being discharged, does so at his peril and will be in contempt if the discharge is refused.[88] The fact that the defendant's non-compliance was based on erroneous advice from his solicitor is no defence to contempt, although it may mitigate the penalty.[89] A defendant who belatedly complies with the order may be held to have purged his contempt, and any punishment pronounced against him remitted.[90] A defendant who is in contempt may be imprisoned[91] or penalised in costs.[92]

A plaintiff who acts in breach of an undertaking given in pursuance of an Anton Piller order will also be in contempt of court, and the court may, in such a case, disallow any further proceedings on the order.[93]

10. Privilege

In *Rank Film Distributors Inc.* v. *Video Information Centre*[94] a defendant's privilege to refuse to answer interrogatories, on the grounds of self incrimination, was applied to interrogatories administered in pursuance of an Anton Piller order. This principle would clearly remove much of the advantage of the order to the plaintiff and seriously

87. See generally Chapter 6 *supra*.
88. *Wardle Fabrics Ltd.* v. *G. Myristis Ltd.* [1984] F.S.R. 263.
89. *H.P.S.I.* v. *Thomas* (1983) 133 N.L.J. 598.
90. *W.E.A. Records Ltd.* v. *Wheeler* (1984) 135 N.L.J. 13 (30 January, Lexis transcript).
91. *Ibid.*
92. *Randolph M. Fields* v. *Watts* (1984) 129 S.J. 67.
93. *Ibid.*
94. [1982] A.C. 380.

hinder the court's process, and Lord Russell remarked:[95]

> In as much as the privilege in question can go a long way in this and other analogous fields to deprive the owner of his just rights to the protection of his property I would welcome legislation . . .; the aim of such legislation should be remove the privilege, while at the same time preventing the use in criminal proceedings of statements which otherwise have been privileged.

The court rejected the proposition that it should order that information, revealed by such interrogatories, should be privileged in any other action, as only the court seized of the other action could determine whether such privilege should apply.[96] Lord Russell's prayer was speedily answered in the form of s.72 of the Supreme Court Act 1981.

This section provides that in the case of (i) proceedings for the infringement of rights pertaining to any intellectual property or for passing off, (ii) proceedings brought to obtain disclosure of information relating to any infringement of such rights or to any passing off and (iii) proceedings brought to prevent any apprehended infringement of such rights or any apprehended passing off,[97] a person shall not be excused from answering any question or from complying with any order made in those proceedings by reason that to do so would tend to expose that person or his or her spouse to proceedings for a related offence or for the recovery of a related penalty.[98] "Intellectual property" in this context means any patent, trade mark, copyright, registered design, technical or commercial information or

95. *Ibid.*, at p. 86.
96. *Cf. Busby* v. *Thorn EMI Video Programmes Ltd.* [1984] 1 N.Z.L.R. 461, where the New Zealand Court of Appeal held that it had common law jurisdiction to forbid the use of material and information revealed in later proceedings.
97. Supreme Court Act 1981, s.72(2).
98. *Ibid.*, s.72(1).

other intellectual property.[99] "Related offence" means first, in the case of proceedings falling within heads (i) or (ii) above, any offence committed by or in the course of the infringement or passing off to which those proceedings relate, or any offence not falling within the above committed in connection with that infringement or passing off, being an offence involving fraud or dishonesty: secondly, in the case of proceedings falling within head (iii) above, any offence revealed by the facts on which the plaintiff relies in those proceedings.[1] The term "any offence" in relation to heading (iii) must be given its literal meaning, and cannot be confined to offences of the type specified as relating to heads (i) and (ii).[2] "Related penalty" means first, in the case of any proceedings falling in heads (i) and (ii) above, any penalty incurred or omitted in connection with the infringement or passing off to which those proceedings relate and secondly, in the case of proceedings falling within head (iii) above, any penalty incurred in respect of any act or omission revealed by the facts on which the plaintiff relies in those proceedings.[3] The section applies to proceedings in the High Court at first instance and on appeal.[4]

To protect the defendant from further penalties the section provides that no answers given as a result of the application of the section and nothing done in compliance with an order as a result of the application of the section shall be admissible against a person or his or her spouse in proceedings for a related offence, or for the recovery of a related penalty.[5] This exception does not apply to proceedings for perjury or contempt of court.[6]

The privilege against self-incrimination thus remains, in respect of proceedings other than those connected with the

99. *Ibid.*, s.72(5).
 1. *Ibid.*
 2. *Universal City Studios Inc.* v. *Hubbard* [1984] 1 All E.R. 661.
 3. Supreme Court Act 1981, s.72(5).
 4. *Ibid.*, s.72(6).
 5. *Ibid.*, s.72(3).
 6. *Ibid.*, s.72(3).

infringement of intellectual property or passing off, as defined in the section and, in view of the wide application of the Anton Piller order, could still represent an important restriction on its enforcement, albeit no case has yet been reported in which such privilege was pleaded. The privilege does not extend to discovery and to incriminating evidence revealed by an Anton Piller search.[7]

11. Appeals

A defendant who is unwilling to accept an Anton Piller order should apply to the judge who granted it, or to another judge at first instance, to discharge it. Although the Court of Appeal has jurisdiction to hear appeals from *ex parte* applications, it will not exercise its jurisdiction on the defendant's application, as an *ex parte* order is, by its nature, provisional until modified or discharged at first instance. An appeal will only be heard from the refusal of the defendant's application for such modification or discharge[8] and where a plaintiff wishes to keep information confidential he should not disclose it to the court in the course of the application.[9] When a defendant makes such an application to discharge, all the material evidence put forward at the *ex parte* application should be made available to him. Neither the plaintiff nor the court should keep back relevant information even though it may be injurious to the plaintiff's case to disclose it and, where a plaintiff wishes to keep information confidential, he should not disclose it to the court in the course of the application. Sir John Donaldson, M.R. in *W.E.A. Records Ltd.* v. *Visions Channel 4 Ltd.*,[10] in commenting on the withholding of

7. *Rank Film Distributors Inc.* v. *Video Information Centre* [1982] A.C . 380.
8. *W.E.A. Records Ltd.* v. *Visions Channel 4 Ltd.* (1984) 135 N.L.J. 13. 30 January (Lexis transcript).
9. *Ibid*.
10. *Ibid*

information from the defendant at first instance, stated:[11]

> I do not know what this information was, but I cannot at the moment visualise any circumstances in which it would be right to give a judge information on an *ex parte* application which cannot at a later stage be revealed to the party affected by the result of the application. Of course, there may be occasions when it is necessary, for example, to conceal the identity of informants, but the judge should then be told that this information cannot be given to him and the judge will then have to make up his mind to what extent he is prepared to rely on information coming from anonymous and unidentifiable sources.

On hearing such an appeal the Court of Appeal will not unscramble an order which has been executed so as to restore the *status quo ante*. As Sir John Donaldson, M.R. also remarked in *W.E.A. Records Ltd.* v. *Visions Channel 4 Ltd.*[12] in relation to such an application:

> I regard this as wholly absurd. The courts are concerned with the administration of justice, not with playing a game of snakes and ladders. If it were now clear that the defendants had suffered any injustice by the making of the order, taking account of all relevant evidence . . . the defendants would have their remedy in the counter-undertaking as to damages.

In considering the defendant's appeal, the court will have regard to all the relevant evidence, and not only to those matters which were before the judge on the *ex parte* application.[13]

A plaintiff who is refused an Anton Piller order on an *ex parte* application may appeal to the Court of Appeal. The hearing on appeal will normally be in open court, but where counsel forms the opinion that the appeal should be heard

11. *Ibid.*, at p. 591.
12. *Ibid.*, at p. 594.
13. *Hallmark Cards Inc.* v. *Image Arts Ltd.* [1977] F.S.R. 150; *W.E.A. Records* v. *Visions Channel 4 Ltd.* (1984) 135 N.L.J. 13. 30 January (Lexis transcript).

in camera he should hand a written and signed statement of his reasons for his opinion to the registrar before the hearing. In doing so, counsel will be expressing his professional opinion, and not the view of his client. The court will then make a preliminary decision on whether the case should be heard *in camera*, thus avoiding the necessity of the reasons for such a hearing being disclosed in open court when the application is made.[14]

12. Discharge

An application may be made to discharge an Anton Piller order before or after execution. If the defendant refuses to permit execution, a subsequent discharge will relieve him from any liability for contempt.[15] If the order has been executed, there seems little advantage in applying for discharge, as any damage done to the defendant's case cannot then be undone, and the defendant will be left to his remedy under the plaintiff's undertaking for damages.[16]

The application for discharge may be based on the failure of the plaintiff to satisfy any of the requirements for the granting of the order. Where the ground alleged is the non-disclosure of material facts by the plaintiff, it will not, assuming there is no evidence of fraud, be sufficient to show that had the judge been in possession of all the material facts he would have reached a different conclusion, and the applicant must adduce evidence that the judge was not fully informed of all the facts relevant to the weighing operation which the court has to make in deciding whether to grant the order.[17] An application to discharge may be made by summons or motion.[18]

14. *Practice Note* [1982] 3 All E.R. 924.
15. *Wardle Fabrics Ltd.* v. *G. Myristis Ltd.* [1984] F.S.R. 263.
16. *W.E.A. Records Ltd.* v. *Visions Channel 4 Ltd.* (1984) 135 N.L.J.13.
17. *Thermax* v. *Schlott Industrial Glass.* [1981] F.S.R. 289.
18. *Thermax* v. *Schlott Industrial Glass* [1981] F.S.R. 289; *Wardle Fabrics* v. *G. Myristis Ltd.* [1984] F.S.R. 263, *Jeffrey Rogers Knitwear Productions Ltd.* v. *Vinola (Knitwear) Manufacturing Co.*, unreported, 23 November, 1984 (Lexis transcript).

13. Enforcement of cross-undertaking in damages

The plaintiff's undertaking in damages may only be enforced when the court has decided not to affirm the injunction or make it permanent, and then the undertaking may only be enforced at the discretion of the court.[19] The undertaking may not be enforced by means of a counterclaim by the defendant before the final judgment of the court as the undertaking is itself an undertaking to the court and does not create any basis of claim, whether in contract or in tort, on which the defendant may proceed against the plaintiff without the court's intervention.[20] The undertaking may not be enforced on the basis that the order has been improperly executed, as this raises an issue totally separate from the claim.[21]

14. Counterclaim for damages on the order

A counterclaim may not be based on the allegation that the obtaining of the order was an abuse of the process of the court unless it can be shown that the order was obtained for an improper purpose, such as to obtain property to which the plaintiffs were not entitled.[22] If the plaintiffs' motive was correct, and the application made to preserve evidence where grounds existed for believing that it would otherwise be destroyed or removed, the defendant's only course is to seek the discharge of the order and the enforcement of the undertaking in damages.[23]

Similarly, where the defendant alleges that the plaintiffs failed to disclose material facts on the *ex parte* application, no claim for damages may be maintained by the defendant, as the plaintiffs' duty is owed to the court, and not to the

19. *Fletcher Sutcliffe Wild Ltd*. v. *Burch* [1982] F.S.R. 64.
20. *Ibid*.
21. *Ibid*.
22. *Digital Equipment Corp*. v. *Darkcrest Ltd*. [1984] 3 All E.R. 381.
23. *Ibid*. As to discharge see p. 113 *supra*. As to the enforcement of the undertaking in damages see p. 13, *supra*.

defendant.[24] Again, an application for discharge and the enforcement of the undertaking is the defendant's only remedy.

15. Costs

The costs of an Anton Piller application will usually be reserved.[25] Where, however, evidence before the court on an *inter partes* hearing indicates that the plaintiffs should not have embarked on their application, at least without making further investigations, the court may direct that there should be no order as to the costs of the application.[26]

The Right of Arrest in Admiralty Jurisdiction

The right to arrest a ship, the proceeds of a sale of a ship, a cargo, or freight arises in the following cases. Firstly, where an action *in rem* is brought in respect of an incident giving rise to a maritime lien. Such a lien will lie against the subject-matter of the claim wherever it may go, even into the hands of a *bona fide* purchaser who knew nothing of the claim at the time of purchase.[27] Secondly, where an action *in rem* arises from any claim against the ship or property in the following cases:[28]

   (a) any claim to the possession or ownership of a ship or any share in a ship.[29]
   (b) any question arising between co-owners of a ship as to the possession, employment or earnings of that ship.[30]

---

24. *Ibid.*
25. *Systematica Ltd.* v. *London Computer Centre Ltd.* [1983] F.S.R. 313.
26. *Ibid.*
27. Supreme Court Act 1981, s.21(3).
28. *Ibid.*, s.21(2).
29. *Ibid.*, s.30(2)(a). This includes the ownership of foreign ships. *The Jupiter* [1925] All E.R. Rep. 203.
30. Supreme Court Act 1981, s. 20(2)(b). See *e.g.*, *The Nellie Schneider* (1878) L.R. 3 P.D. 152.

(c) any claim in respect of a mortgage or charge on a ship or any share in a ship,[31] whether the mortgage is registered or unregistered, legal or equitable, or created under English or foreign Law.[32]

(d) any claim for the forfeiture or condemnation of a ship or of goods which are being or have been carried, or have been attempted to be carried, in a ship, or for the restoration of a ship or any such goods after seizure, or for droits of the Admiralty.[33]

Thirdly, where a claim *in rem* arises in connection with a ship, and the person who would be liable on the claim, if an action *in personam* (the relevant person) were brought, was the owner or charterer, or in possession or control of the ship when the action arose in the following cases:[34]

(a) any claim for damage done by a ship;[35] including any claim in respect of liability incurred under the Merchant Shipping (Oil Pollution) Act 1971 and in respect of any liability falling on the International Oil Pollution Compensation Fund under Part I of the Merchant Shipping Act 1974, and any claim in respect of damage done to foreign land or property.[36]

(b) any claim for loss of life or personal injury sustained in consequence of any defect in a ship or in her apparel or equipment, or of the wrongful act, negligence or default of the owners, charterers or persons in possession or control of the ship, or of the master or crew or of any other persons for whose wrongful acts, neglects or defaults the owners, charterers or persons in possession or control are responsible being an act of neglect or default in the navigation or management of the ship, in the loading

---

31. Supreme Court Act 1981, s.20(2)(c).
32. *Ibid.*, s.20(7)(c) *The Acrux* [1965] 1 Lloyd's Rep. 5a 65.
33. *Ibid.*, s.20(2)(s).
34. *Ibid.*, s.21(4).
35. *Ibid.*, s.20(2)(e).
36. *Ibid.*, s.20(5).

carriage or disembarkation of persons on, in or from the ship.[37]

(c) any claim for loss or damage to goods carried in a ship, where brought by the owners of those goods.[38]

(d) any claim arising out of any agreement relating to the carriage of goods on a ship or to the use or hire of a ship.[39]

(e) any claim in the nature of salvage.[40]

(f) any claim in the nature of towage in respect of a ship or an aircraft.[41]

(g) any claim in the nature of pilotage in respect of a ship or aircraft.[42]

(h) any claim in respect of goods or materials supplied to a ship for her operation or maintenance.[43]

(i) any claim in respect of construction repair or equipment of a ship or dock charges or dues.[44]

(j) any claim by a master or a member of the crew of a ship for wages (including any sum allotted out of wages or adjudged by a superintendent to be due by way of wages,[45] and including wages claimed by the master and crew of a foreign vessel.[46]

(k) any claim by a master, shipper, charterer or agent in respect of disbursements made on account of a ship.[47]

37. *Ibid.*, s.20(2)(f).
38. *Ibid.*, s.20(2((g). See also *The Eschersheim* [1976] 2 Lloyd's Rep. 1.
39. *Ibid.*, s.20(2)(h). This has been held to cover salvage agreements; *The Eschersheim* [1976] 2 Lloyd's Rep. 1 and indemnity agreements in a towage contract; *The Conoco Britannia* [1972] 1 Lloyd's Rep. 342.
40. *Ibid.*, s.20(2)(j).
41. *Ibid.*, s.20(2)(k).
42. *Ibid.*, s.(2)(2)(1).
43. *Ibid.*, s.20(2)(m). This includes monies paid for necessaries. *The Fairport (No. 5)* [1967] 2 Lloyd's Rep. 187.
44. *Ibid.*, s.20(2)(n). 'Equipment' does not include fuel. *The D'Vora* [1952] 2 Lloyd's Rep. 404.
45. *Ibid.*, s.20(2)(o).
46. *Ibid.*, s.24(2)(a).
47. *Ibid.*, s.20(2)(p).

(l) any claim arising out of an act which is or is claimed to be a general average act.[48]

(m) any claim arising out of bottomry.[49]

In the first and third cases above, the right of arrest extends to any other ship in which the relevant person is the full beneficial owner at the time the cause of action arose,[50] albeit the court's jurisdiction may be exercised before strict proof of this requirement has been made.[51]

The arrest may be made under a warrant issued by the Admiralty Marshal on the basis of the writ,[52] and will be effected by attaching the writ or warrant to the vessel or cargo against which the action is brought, as specified in R.S.C. Ord. 75.[53]

The *res* will be released from arrest where the defendant provides bail[54] or, as is more usual in practice, agrees to provide security for the plaintiff's claim.[55] The *res* may, after judgment, be sold by the order of the court and the proceeds applied to the satisfaction of the claim.[56] The court has jurisdiction to decide any question of priorities amongst claims to the proceeds[57] and to hear claims by way of intervention from persons claiming an interest in the *res* or proceeds.[58]

By making the specific *res* available for the satisfaction of a successful judgment, the arrest procedure appears, at first sight, to have considerable advantage over other procedures. Whether, in practice, this is correct, however, is

---

48. *Ibid.*, s.20(2)(q).
49. *Ibid.*, s.20(2)(r).
50. *Ibid.*, s.21(4).
51. *The Elefteria* [1957] 2 All E.R. 374.
52. R.S.C. Ord. 75 r. 5.
53. *Ibid.*, r. 11, which also covers arrest in respect of freight and cargo which has been transshipped.
54. Cf. R.S.C. Ord. 75 r.16.
55. *Cf. The Gay Tucan* [1968] 2 Lloyd's Rep. 245.
56. R.S.C. Ord. 75 r. 23.
57. *Ibid.*, r. 24.
58. *Ibid.*, r.17.

open to doubt. In *The Span Terza*[59] Donaldson, L.J., in the course of argument, suggested to counsel for the appellants that his cause, which he sought to protect by means of a sister ship arrest, would be equally well served by a Mareva injunction, as it would be just as effective in preventing the respondents from removing the vessel from the jurisdiction. Commenting on counsel's refusal to change his application, his Lordship said:[60]

> (Counsel) was unable to tell me why he preferred to arrest this ship, rather than to obtain an injunction preventing the owners from taking it out of the jurisdiction, which must inevitably have led to the provision of security in exactly the same way as security will, no doubt, be provided in respect of this arrest — he was unable to tell me why his clients took that view — and it would of course have been wrong of me to have pressed him, intrigued though I was and still am.

Be that as it may, the power of arrest is still clearly one of great importance within Admiralty jurisdiction, particularly as the jurisdiction to arrest, and the jurisdiction to grant a Mareva injunction are far from co-extensive.[61]

---

59. [1981] 1 Lloyd's Rep. 225.
60. *Ibid.*, at p. 229.
61. See the remarks of Sheen, J. in *The Tuyuti* [1984] 2 Lloyd's. Rep. 51.

CHAPTER 8

PRE-TRIAL RIGHTS IN OTHER JURISDICTIONS

Two major matters will be considered in this chapter. First, the acceptance of the Mareva injunction in other jurisdictions, and some of the problems faced thereby. Secondly, the main types of pre-trial arrest or attachment widely used in civil law jurisdictions, and in some common law jurisdictions where statutory provision is sometimes made, and in Scots and Roman-Dutch law, where the remedy of arrestment *ad fundandum jurisdictionem* is used to found jurisdiction as well as provide security.

Mareva Injunction in other Jurisdictions

1. Australia

In Australia the Mareva jurisdiction was accepted in Queensland,[1] Victoria[2] and Western Australia,[3] the jurisdiction being based on legislation equivalent to that of s.45 of the Supreme Court of Judicature (Consolidation) Act 1925. In South Australia and New South Wales the jurisdiction was rejected in early cases, the courts strongly rejecting the concept that what they regarded as a form of pre-trial attachment should be incorporated into the law other than by means of legislation.[4] More recently, however, the jurisdiction has been accepted in New South

1. *Hunt* v. *B.P. Exploration Co. (Libya) Ltd.* (1980) 28 A.L.R. 145. *Bank of New Zealand* v. *Jones* [1982] Qd. R. 466.
2. *Praznovsky* v. *Salblyack* [1978] V.R. 185.
3. *Sanko Steamship Co. Ltd.* v. *D.C. Commodities (A'Asia) Ltd.* [1980] W.A.R. 51.
4. *Pivovaroff* v. *Chernabaeff* (1978) 16 S.A.S.R. 329; see especially the judgment of Bray, C. J. at p. 340; *Ex parte B.P. Exploration Co. (Libya) Ltd., Re Hunt* [1979] 2 N.S.W.L.R. 406.

Wales.[5] The jurisdiction has also been accepted by the courts of the Australian Capital Territories,[6] the High Court of Australia[7] and the Federal Court of Australia.[8] The courts have accepted the general principles of the Mareva injunction as laid down in the *Mareva*,[9] *Pertamina*[10] and *Siskina*[11] cases, the jurisdiction to retain home-based defendants by means of the order[12] and to apply it to the dissipation of assets within the jurisdiction, as well as their removal from it.[13] A Mareva injunction may be varied to release funds for the defendant's legitimate purposes, but this will require proof that there are no other assets available to the defendant from which he could satisfy or accomplish those purposes.[14]

2. Canada

The jurisdiction to grant a Mareva injunction has been accepted in most provinces including North West Territories,[15] Ontario,[16] New Brunswick,[17] Nova Scotia,[18]

5. *Turner* v. *Sylvester* [1981] 2 N.S.W.L.R. 295; *Riley McKay Pty Ltd.* v. *McKay* [1982] 1 N.S.W.L.R. 264; *Australian Iron and Steel Pty Ltd.* v. *Buck* [1982] 2 N.S.W.L.R. 889.
6. *Barisic* v. *Topic* (1981) 37 A.C.T.R. 1.
7. *Hunt* v. *B.P. Exploration (Libya) Ltd.* (1980) 28 A.L.R. 145.
8. *Hiero Pty. Ltd.* v. *Somers* (1983) 47 A.L.R. 506.
9. *Mareva Compania Naviera SA* v. *International Bulkcarriers SA* [1975] 2 Lloyd's Rep. 509.
10. *Rasu Maritima SA* v. *Perushaan Pertambangan Minak Dan Gas Bumi Negara* [1978] Q.B. 644, [1977] 3 All E.R. 803, [1977] 3 W.W.R. 518.
11. *The Siskina* [1979] A.C. 210, [1977] 3 All E.R. 803, [1978] 1 Lloyd's Rep. 1.
12. *Turner* v. *Sylvester, supra. Riley McKay Pty Ltd.* v. *McKay* [1981] 2 N.S.W.L.R. 295.
13. *Australian Iron and Steel Pty Ltd.* v. *Buck* [1982] 2 N.S.W.L.R. 889.
14. *Ibid.*
15. *Hunt* v. *B.P. Exploration Co. (Libya) Ltd.* (1981) 114 D.L.R. (3d) 35.
16. *Liberty National Bank and Trust Co.* v. *Atkin* (1981) 12 D.L.R. (3d) 160; *Canadian Pacific Airlines Ltd.* v. *Hind* (1981) 122 D.L.R. (3d) 498; *Chitel* v. *Rothbart* (1982) 141 D.L.R. (3d) 268.
17. *Humphreys* v. *Buraglia* (1982) 135 D.L.R. (3d) 535.
18. *Parmar Fisheries Ltd.* v. *Parceria Maritima Esperance L. DA.* (1982) 141 D.L.R. 498.

Manitoba,[19] British Columbia[20] and in the Federal Court.[21] In Nova Scotia and Manitoba it has been held that this jurisdiction may be exercised despite the existence of a statutory right of pre-trial attachment.[22]

It has been emphasised that the Mareva injunction is essentially an exception to the general rule in *Lister* v. *Stubbs*,[23] and that the courts should be at pains to guard against abuse of the jurisdiction.[24] The guidelines set out in *Third Chandris Shipping Corp.* v. *Unimarine SA, The Genie*[25] have been accepted by various courts,[26] and the need for the plaintiff to adduce adequate evidence in support of his claim[27] and to make full and frank disclosure,[28] have been stressed. Applications have been permitted against defendants within the jurisdiction in New Brunswick,[29] but doubts as to whether the jurisdiction should be extended to permit this have been expressed in Ontario.[30]

19. *Feigelman* v. *Aetna Financial Services Ltd.* (1982) 143 D.L.R. (3d) 715.
20. *Manousakis* v. *Manousakis* (1979) 10 B.C.L.R. 21.
21. *Elesgara Inc.* v. *Ssangyong Shipping* (1980) 117 D.L.R. (3d) 105.
22. *Parmar Fisheries Ltd.* v. *Parceria Maritima Esperanca L. DA.* (1982) 141 D.L.R. (3d) 498; *Feigelman* v. *Aetna Financial Services Ltd.* (1982). 143 D.L.R. (3d) 715. In both cases it was accepted that there was a statutory basis analogous with s.45 of the Supreme Court of Judicature (Consolidation) Act 1925, for the jurisdiction to make the Mareva injunction.
23. [1890] 45 Ch.D. 1.
24. *Canadian Pacific Airlines Ltd.* v. *Hind* (1981) 122 D.L.R. (3d) 498; *Chitel* v. *Rothbart* (1982) 141 D.L.R. (3d) 268.
25. [1979] 2 All E.R. 972, [1979] 2 Lloyd's Rep 194.
26. *Chitel* v. *Rothbart* (1982) 141 D.L.R. (3d) 268, Ontario Court of Appeal; *Parmar Fisheries Ltd.* v. *Parceria Maritima Esperanca L. DA.* (1982) 141 D.L.R. (3d) 498, Novia Scotia Supreme Court.
27. *Chitel* v. *Rothbart* (1982) 141 D.L.R. (3d) 268.
28. *Ibid. Humphreys* v. *Burgalia* (1982) 135 D.L.R. (3d) 535.
29. *Humphreys* v. *Burgalia* (1982) 135 D.L.R. (3d) 535.
30. *Quinn* v. *Marsta Cession Services* (1981) 133 D.L.R. (3d) 109 at p. 113. *Cf.* the judgment of MacKinnon, A.C.J.O. in *Chitel* v. *Rothbart* (1982) 141 D.L.R. (3d) 268, at pp. 285–6.

3. Hong Kong

The jurisdiction to grant a Mareva injunction in accordance with English law principles has been accepted in Hong Kong,[31] notwithstanding the s.37 of the Supreme Court Act 1981 has not been enacted there.[37] The Mareva jurisdiction has been applied to actions for unliquidated damages.[33]

4. Malaysia

The Mareva jurisdiction has been accepted in Malaya[34] and Singapore[35] on the basis that there exists legislation equivalent to s.45 of the Supreme Court of Judicature (Consolidation) Act 1925, and English law principles have been applied. In Brunei, the jurisdiction has not been accepted owing to the lack of equivalent enabling legislation.[36]

5. New Zealand

The Mareva jurisdiction has been accepted in New Zealand[37] and English law principles have been applied, but doubt has been expressed as to whether the jurisdiction would extend to a defendant within the jurisdiction.[38]

31. *Chen Lee Hong-man* v. *William Chen* [1981] H.K.L.R. 176; *Union Carbide Corp.* v. *Hing Luis Offset Printing Co.* [1981] F.S.R. 109.
32. *American Express International Banking Corp.* v. *Willie Yu* [1983] H.K.L.R. 148. Discretion to grant the remedy is given under Ord. 19 Supreme Court Ordinance, Cap. 4.
33. *Chen Lee Hong-man* v. *William Chen* [1981] H.K.L.R. 176.
34. *Zainin Abidin Bin Haji Abdul Rahman* v. *Century Hotels Sdn. Bhd.* [1982] 1 M.L.J. 260.
35. *Art Trend Ltd.* v. *Blue Dolphin (Pte)* [1983] 2 M.L.J. 93.
36. *Mohmmed Hassan* v. *Sherwood Bears (S) Pte Ltd.* [1983] 2 M.L.J. 420.
37. *Systems and Programmes (NZ) Ltd.* v. *PRC Public Management Services (Inc)*, unreported 5 April, 1978; *Mosen* v. *Donelaar*, unreported 13 October, 1978; *Hunt* v. *B.P. Exploration Co. (Libya) Ltd.* (1980) 28 A.L.R. 145, [1980] N.Z.L.R. 104.
38. *Mayall* v. *Weal* [1982] 2 N.Z.L.R. 385.

6. *Arrestment ad fundandum jurisdictionem*

The *arrestment ad fundandum jurisdictionem* has two functions, to establish the jurisdiction of the court, and to provide security for judgment. In Scotland, the arrestment of movables belonging to the defendant in the hands of the defendant or of a third party, will enable the pursuer to establish the jurisdiction of the Scottish courts in a case against the defender.[39] In South Africa, attachment of the person or property of a *peregrini* defendant, where the plaintiff is an *incola*, has been required to establish jurisdiction first, where the cause of action arises within the court's jurisdiction and secondly, in cases where the court has no basis of jurisdiction other than the arrest of the defendant's person or property.[40] The first of these two cases is, strictly speaking, an *arrestment ad confirmandum jurisdictionem*, as the right of jurisdiction exists independently of the arrest, the distinction being important in certain statutory provisions, but the term *arrestment ad fundandum jurisdictionem* is usually applied to both. In the second case, there is no need to show any independent basis of jurisdiction, the arrestment itself being sufficient.[41] Such an arrestment cannot be made at the suit of a *peregrini* plaintiff, although such a plaintiff may seek an *arrestment ad confirmandum jurisdictionem*.[42] In the case where *arrestment ad fundandum jurisdictionem* is necessary, the nature of the proceedings is irrelevant, and may be in contract or in delict, provided that the plaintiff's claim sounds in money. The right to order such attachment is based on the doctrine of effectiveness, *i.e.*, so that effect may be given to the

---

39. See Walker, *Principles of Scottish Private Law* 3rd ed.
40. *Einwald* v. *German West African Co.* 5 Sc. 86.
41. *Lecomte* v. *W. & B. Syndicate of Madagascar* (1905) T.S. 696; *Bradbury Gretorex Co. (Colonial) Ltd.* v. *Standard Trading Co. (Pty) Ltd.* [1953] 3 S.A.L.R. 529; *Central African Airways Corp.* v. *Vickers Armstrong Ltd.* [1956] 2 S.A.L.R. 492. *Murphy* v. *Dallas* [1974] 1 S.A.L.R. 793.
42. *Nolan* v. *Master of SS "Russel Haverside"* [1921] C.P.D. 136.

court's ultimate order. It has been pointed out, however, that this doctrine does not literally require that the property arrested have an equivalent value to the sum claimed, and an order may be made in respect of any property which has a commercial value.[43]

Attachment may be made of any property within the jurisdiction belonging to the defendant, whether movable[44] or immovable[45] even, in the latter case, where goods are subject to a lien or pledge.[46] Movable property must, as well as belonging to the defendant, be in his possession or that of his agent.[47] Attachment may also be granted against incorporeal rights, such as rights under an inheritance,[48] shares[49] and dividends due from an insolvent estate.[50] The plaintiff should make out a *prima facie* case in support of his claim before attachment will be ordered, but this means, in practice, that the application will only be refused or discharged when it can be shown that the plaintiff has no cause of action.[51] It has been pointed out in some cases, however, that the remedy is not discretionary, and as long as the plaintiff can fulfil the basic requirements he is entitled to it as of right.[52] Nevertheless, the courts have emphasised the need for care and caution in view of the exceptional nature of the remedy.[53]

43. *Thermo Radiant Oven Sales (Pty) Ltd.* v. *Nelspruit Bakeries (Pty) Ltd.* [1969] 2 S.A.L.R. 295.
44. *Ex parte Rehbock* [1879] K. 103; *Ex parte Wellington Co-operative Fruit Growers Ltd.* 20 C.T.R. 979.
45. *Potgeiter* v. *Blunden* 8 H.C.G. 133.
46. *London Bank of Australia* v. *Paarl Roller Mills* [1921] C.P.D. 354; *Ex parte Southern Lands* [1921] C.P.D. 150. *Hymore Agencies Durban (Pty) Ltd.* v. *Gin Nih Weaving Factory* [1959] 1 S.A.L.R. 180.
47. *Ex parte Rehbock* [1879] K. 103.
48. *Barkhuysten* v. *Van Huysten* 1 S.C. 26.
49. *Rand Estate Agency (Pty) Ltd.* v. *Lacey* [1949] 4 S.A.L.R. 83.
50. *Landau Bros.* v. *C. de Giavanni & Son* [1914] S.R. 36.
51. *Lecomte* v. *W. & B. Syndicate of Madagascar*, (1905) T.S. 696. *Bradbury* v. *Gretorex Co. (Colonial) Ltd.* v. *Standard Trading Co. (Pty) Ltd.* [1953] 3 S.A.L.R. 529.
52. *Jackaman* v. *Arkell* [1953] 3 S.A.L.R. 31.
53. *Ex parte Acrow Engineers (Pty) Ltd.* [1953] 2 S.A. 319.

A defendant subject to an order of arrestment may obtain the release of his property by giving security to the value of the plaintiff's claim together with the costs of the application of attachment.[54]

A defendant who takes this course may not later be compelled to give further security.[55] A defendant may also apply for the discharge of the order of arrestment on the ground that the requirements for a valid arrestment have not been met. Thus, discharge may be granted where the defendant can show that he is an *incola* and not a *peregrinus*,[56] or that the plaintiff has no *prima facie* case.[57]

RIGHTS OF ARREST AND ATTACHMENT

In most civil law, and in some common law jurisdictions, examples from which are cited below, provision is made, by code or by statute, for the arrest or attachment of the defendant's property at the interlocutory stage of the proceedings. Such rights, in many cases, approximate to the right *in rem* exercised in English Admiralty jurisdiction, although in most civil law jurisdictions the distinction between rights *in rem* and rights *in personam* is not recognised in the same way as at common law. In the United States, however, where the old Law Merchant remedy of "foreign attachment" was recognised from early times, albeit the right now depends on statutory jurisdiction in each state where it can be exercised, the right is not purely *in rem*, but more of a hybrid between *in rem* and *in personam* actions.

The validity of such rights of arrest and attachment have been accepted unchallenged into the jurisprudence of most

---

54. *Thompson Watson & Co.* v. *Poverty Bay Farmers' Meat Supply Co.* [1924] C.P.D. 93.
55. *Ibid.*
56. *Kehmann* v. *Weiss* [1935] S.W.A. 33.
57. *Lippert* v. *De Marrillac* 11 S.C. 312.

countries where they are exercised. In the United States, however, it has been argued that such a pre-trial deprivation of the defendant's property transgresses the fifth and fourteenth Amendments to the U.S. Constitution, both of which seek to ensure, *inter alia*, that no person should be deprived of his property without due process of law. Seizure of property without trial and without the defendant being given an opportunity to be heard has been held to violate "due process" in both State[58] and Federal courts,[59] although the decisions depend on the wording of the individual statutes concerned. The Federal Supreme Court decision in *Schaffer* v. *Heitner*[60] however, leaves open the way for such arrest provided the parties have a sufficient contact with the jurisdiction of the state concerned to satisfy the requirement that "fair play and substantial justice" be done.[61] Similarly, the right of arrest of vessels under Supplementary Admiralty Rules B and C[62] has been accepted subject to certain safeguards.[63]

The high water mark of a plaintiff's protection may be seen in French law with its array of such remedies, in particular, *saisie arrete*,[64] enabling the plaintiff to garnish

---

58. From amongst the voluminous sources, recent examples can be found in Georgia, *Johnson* v. *American Credit Co. of Georgia*, 581 F 2d 526; Mississippi, *M.P.I. Inc.* v. *McCullough* 463 F. Supp. 887; and Vermont, *Briere* v. *Agway Inc.* 425 F. Supp. 654. Many others are included in the Decentennial Digests.
59. *Sniadach* v. *Family Finance Corp.* 395 U.S. 337, 23 L. Ed. 2d 347 (1969).
60. 433 U.S. 186, 53 L. Ed. 2d. 683 (1977).
61. See Marshall, J.'s comments, *ibid.*, at pp. 202–5 and 697–8 and at pp. 207–10 and 699–701. See also *International Shoe Co.* v. *Washington* 326 U.S. 310, 90 L.Ed. 95 (1945).
62. Supplemental Rule B. Attachment and Garnishment. Supplemental Rule C. Actions in rem. 28 US Code. Supplemental Rules for Certain Admiralty and Maritime Claims.
63. *Grand Bahama Petroleum* v. *Canadian Transport Agencies* [1978] A.M.C. 789, and note the authorities and the guidelines collected by Tetley, *Attachment, the Mareva injunction and saisie conservatoire*, [1985] L.M.C.L.Q. 58 at pp. 62–3.
64. See Code de Procedure Civil, Arts. 557–582.

property in the hands of a third party, *saisie conservatoire*,[65] giving the plaintiff a general right of arrest over the defendant's property, and *saisie foraine*,[66] giving the plaintiff a right of arrest over the defendant's property situated within a jurisdiction in which the defendant is neither resident or domiciled.

The *saisie conservatoire*, the most versatile and widely used of these remedies, is, in many ways, similar to an action *in rem* in English law. The property concerned may be seized in any action in which the court has jurisdiction, the main pre-conditions being that the case is one of urgency and that the recovery of the debt appears to be in peril. However, as in most provisions for arrest, there need be no connection between the property seized and the substantive matter of the claim.[67]

Several other jurisdictions provide a similar right, albeit in more restricted circumstances. In Germany and in Sweden, the applicant must show there exists a likelihood that the defendant will take steps to frustrate the judgment,[68] whereas in Spain, arrest is available only where the defendant is not a Spanish national, or is not resident or domiciled in Spain, or where evidence can be adduced to show that the defendant is likely to abscond or remove his assets from the jurisdiction.[69] In Japan, provisional attachment is available against any property of the defendant, whether or not he is domiciled or resident in Japan. The plaintiff must show that if the attachment is not granted, execution of the judgment will be rendered impossible or extremely difficult. Alternatively, the plaintiff may seek attachment where the bulk of the defendant's property is

65. *Ibid.*, Art. 48. A similar remedy is available in Quebec, see Quebec Code of Civil Procedure, Arts. 773–789.
66. Code de Procedure Civil, Arts 819–821.
67. *Ibid.*, Art. 48.
68. Zivilprozessordnung, s.916 et seq. Rattegangsblat, June 18, 1942, Ch. 15.
69. Enjuiciamiento Civil 1984. Titulo XIV de los embargos preventiovos y del assegguramiento de los bienes litigios, Arts. 1397–1418.

outside the jurisdiction, or there is a danger that the defendant may remove it.[70]

Similar examples can be found in statutory provisions for arrest in Common Law jurisdictions. Thus, in Nova Scotia,[71] a right of arrest is provided where the defendant resides outside the jurisdiction, or is a corporation not registered within the jurisdiction and is about to remove or has removed property permanently out of the jurisdiction. In Manitoba,[72] an attachment can be made where the defendant, being a resident of Manitoba, leaves the jurisdiction or conceals himself within it, with intent to defraud his creditors; or where he is not a resident, is legally liable in an action within the jurisdiction; or, whether or not he is a resident, is about to transfer his property out of the jurisdiction or otherwise dispose of it to delay, defeat or defraud his creditors.

The right of attachment in the U.S.A., where the common law distinction between rights *in rem* and other rights has been drawn, has been held not to be a true right *in rem* (albeit, rights *in rem* exist in Admiralty jurisdiction), but has been described as a right '*quasi in rem*' as the order operates against the defendant personally, albeit it attaches to his property to create a lien in favour of the plaintiff conditional on the plaintiff succeeding in his action.[73] The right does not travel with the property when it comes into other hands in the same way as an order of arrest. The conditions for obtaining an order of attachment depend on the wording of the statute of the state in whose jurisdiction the order is sought, some statutes, for example, requiring evidence that the property will be removed,[74] some requiring that the plaintiff show the defendant is likely to

---

70. Code of Civil Procedure Art. 738.
71. Civil Procedure Rules, Rule 49.
72. Court Rules, Rule 582.
73. *e.g., Bray* v. *McClurry* 55 Mo. 128; *Bolling* v. *Pikeville National Bank* 280 S.W. 1090.
74. *e.g., Bowman* v. *Dussault* 425 A. 2d. 1325.

remove the property with the fraudulent intent of defeating execution of judgment.[75] The requirements of the statute must be discharged on the basis of the reasonable possibility of the dependant's future conduct.[76]

An order of arrest or attachment may, in some jurisdictions, be made both by the court seized of the trial of the action and by an inferior court having sufficient jurisdiction over the defendant or his property, so that the urgency of the case may be met. Thus, in France, application may be made to a *tribunal d'instance* in whose jurisdiction the defendant is domiciled or the property is situated, as well as to the *tribunal de grande instance*.[77] In Germany, jurisdiction is vested in the *Amtsgericht*, in whose jurisdiction the property is situated, as well as in the *Gericht der Hauptsache*.[78] Similarly, in Japan, an order may be made by the district court seized of the case, or by the court within whose jurisdiction the property is situated.[79] In the case of attachment in the U.S.A., the statute will provide which courts in the state have jurisdiction.

Most jurisdictions place some requirement on the plaintiff to demonstrate that he has a case against the defendant. In France and in Germany, the plaintiff must show that he has a valid cause of action against the defendant within the jurisdiction of the court seized of the trial,[80] albeit in practice this often amounts to little more than showing that the plaintiff has commenced, or intends shortly to commence, an action against the defendant and can produce affidavit evidence to support the application.

In Sweden, on the other hand, the plaintiff must show that he has an arguable claim against the defendant.[81] In

---

75. *e.g.*, *Carney* v. *Security Credit Corp.* 135 So. 915.
76. *Bowman* v. *Dussault* 425 A. 2d. 1325, applying Rule 4A, Rules of Civil Procedure (Me).
77. Code de Procedure Civil, Art. 48.
78. Zivilprozessordnung, s.919. The existence of property in Germany is sufficient to give the courts jurisdiction. Zivilprozessordnung, s.23.
79. CCP Art. 739.
80. *E.g.* Code de Procedure Civil Art. 48. ZPO s.197.
81. Rattegangsbalk, Ch. 15.

respect of attachment, it seems generally that a writ must be issued, but that other conditions may be laid down in the statute invoked.[82]

In Japan, the submission of a statement of claim together with a statement of facts supporting the need for an order must be submitted to the court, whereupon the court may make an order without hearing any oral evidence or submissions.[83] The statement in support of the application must, however, be based on objective criteria, so as to highlight such factual matters as the previous behaviour of the defendant, rather than upon the subjective fears of the plaintiff.[84] Further, the application will be refused if the plaintiff already has sufficient security or adequate alternative means to pursue execution.[85]

The scope of the claims covered varies from one jurisdiction to another. In France, Germany and Japan, arrest is limited to claims for money or which can be expressed in terms of money,[86] whereas in many cases of attachment a wider range of claims may be entertained,[87] albeit in claims for specific performance, attachment is not usually available.[88] Arrest may be exercised over most forms of movable property, and may be extended to cover realty, albeit the right in such case may be of limited duration.[89] In all jurisdictions the seizure is carried out under the auspices of the court, and the plaintiff is not empowered to physically enter the defendant's premises and seize the property for himself. Physical custody of the

82. *Cf. Bird.* v. *Dawkins* 6 L.A. App 244.
83. CCP Arts. 740, 741.
84. *Ibid.*, Arts. 737, 738.
85. *Ibid.*
86. *Cf. Prevost* v. *Bottos Cour Paris.* May 5 1959 [1959] D.J. 304. As to the extent to which unliquidated claims may be secured see Herzog, *Civil Procedure in France* p. 235. In Japan see, CCP Art. 737.
87. This is entirely dependent on the wording of the statute invoked.
88. *E.g. Ebsury Gypsum Co.* v. *Ruby* 176 NE 820.
89. Code de Procedure Civil Art. 54. Note also the right to register a lien over a business given by Art. 53.

property is not always necessary to enforce the arrest. In France and Sweden, the property may be left in the custody of the defendant; in France, with the consent of the parties,[90] and in Sweden where the court orders the property to be appropriately labelled by the arresting officer.[91] In Japan, the attachment must be exercised within fourteen days of the order being made.[92]

In most jurisdictions, the arrest and attachment procedures may be invoked prior to the commencement of the action, in which case the order will usually be conditional on the action being commenced within a specified time.[93] Many jurisdictions also require security from the plaintiff, sometimes in the form of a bond, to ensure the defendant will receive adequate compensation if the action fails. In France, however, such security is not mandatory.[94]

Most jurisdictions also provide that the defendant may seek the discharge of the order of arrest or attachment by showing that the court has no jurisdiction,[95] or that the plaintiff cannot satisfy the requirements for the making of an order,[96] or by giving security for the plaintiff's claim.[97]

Certain jurisdictions provide additional or alternative interlocutory remedies to protect the plaintiff's position. In Japan, two forms of injunctive remedy are recognised within the remedy of provisional disposition, and may be exercised on the basis that without an order for such a remedy, the judgment would be impossible or very difficult to enforce.[98] First, the defendant may be temporarily prohibited from transferring his property to a third party

90. *Ibid.*, Arts. 51–52.
91. Utsokningslag, Art. 74.
92. Civil Execution Law Arts. 174–178.
93. Code de Procedure Civil Art. 48. Zivilprozessordnung, s. 926. CCP Art. 746.
94. Code de Procedure Civil Art. 48. Cf. CCP Art. 741.
95. Code de Procedure Civil, Art. 48. Zivilprozessordnung, ss.924, 927.
96. *Ibid.* See also CCP Art. 744.
97. Code de Procedure Civil, Art. 50. Zivilprozessordnung, s.923.
98. CCP Arts 755, 756.

and be required to maintain the *status quo*, as regards the property, until judgment.[99] Any property of the defendant may abe affected by the order.[1] Secondly, an order may be sought to maintain the legal *status quo* between the parties, so that the conduct of one will not be unduly prejudicial to the other.[2] Such an order may, for example, restrain the continued infringement of a copyright or trademark, or provide for the continued employment of an employee, and may be loosely compared with interim injunctions in English law.

In Germany[3] and Sweden,[4] the defendant may be arrested, or at least confined to the territory of the court's jurisdiction, if this is the only way of protecting the potential fruits of judgment. In both these jurisdictions, injunctive remedies are also available; in Sweden, where the risk to the enforcement of judgment is not sufficient to merit arrest,[5] and in Germany in cases where the right of arrest does not apply.[6] This supplemental use of the injunctive remedy may be contrasted with the position in some Canadian Provinces, where the Mareva jurisdiction has been held to exist concurrently, and largely co-extensively with the statutory rights of arrest,[7] and in England, where the Mareva injunction exists in Admiralty jurisdiction alongside the action *in rem*, so that in all these jurisdictions the plaintiff may have a choice of arresting the goods or *res*, or proceeding *in personam* against the defendant. In many instances, the security thus gained will be equally effective.[8]

99. *Ibid.*, Art. 758.
 1. *Ibid.*, Arts 755, 756.
 2. *Ibid.*, Art. 760.
 3. Zivilprozessordnung, s.918.
 4. Strafflag, Ch. 38.
 5. Rattegangsbalk, Ch. 15.
 6. Examples may be found in Zivilprozessordnung, ss. 927, 938 and 940.
 7. *Parmar Fisheries Ltd.* v. *Parceria Maritima Esperenca L.D.A.* (1982) 141 D.L.R. (3d) 498; *Feigelman* v. *Aetna Financial Services Ltd.* (1982) 143 D.L.R. (3d) 715.
 8. Note the comments of Donaldson, L.J., as he then was, in *The Span Terza* [1982] 1 Lloyd's Rep. 225 at p. 229.

APPENDICES

APPENDIX I
SUPREME COURT ACT 1981 c.54
SECTION 37(1)–(3)

37.–(1) The High Court may by order (whether interlocutory or final) grant an injunction or appoint a receiver in all cases in which it appears to the court to be just and convenient to do so.

(2) Any such order may be made either unconditionally or on such terms and conditions as the court thinks just.

(3) The power of the High Court under subsection (1) to grant an interlocutory injunction restraining a party to any proceedings from removing from the jurisdiction of the High Court, or otherwise dealing with, assets located within that jurisdiction shall be exercisable in cases where that party is, as well as in cases where he is not, domiciled, resident or present within that jurisdiction.

APPENDIX II
CIVIL JURISDICTION AND JUDGMENTS ACT 1982
c.27
SECTIONS 24 and 25
SCHEDULE I. ART. 1.

24.–(1) Any power of a court in England and Wales or Northern Ireland to grant interim relief pending trial or pending the determination of an appeal shall extend to a case where:

(a) the issue to be tried, or which is the subject of the appeal, relates to the jurisdiction of the court to entertain the proceedings; or

(b) the proceedings involve the reference of any matter to the European Court under the 1971 Protocol.

(2) Any power of a court in Scotland to grant protective measures pending the decision of any hearing shall apply to a case where:

(a) the subject of the proceedings includes a question as to the jurisdiction of the court to entertain them; or

(b) the proceedings involve the reference of a matter to the European Court under the 1971 Protocol.

(3) Subsections (1) and (2) shall not be construed as restricting any power to grant interim relief or protective measures which a court may have apart from this section.

25.–(1) The High Court in England and Wales or Northern Ireland shall have power to grant interim relief where:

(a) proceedings have been or are to be commenced in a Contracting State other than the United Kingdom or in a part of the United Kingdom other than that in which the High Court in question exercises jurisdiction; and

(b) they are or will be proceedings whose subject-matter is within the scope of the 1968 Convention as determined by Article 1 (whether or not the Convention has effect in relation to the proceedings).

(2) On an application for any interim relief under sub-

section (1) the court may refuse to grant that relief if, in the opinion of the court, the fact that the court has no jurisdiction apart from this section in relation to the subject-matter of the proceedings in question makes it inexpedient for the court to grant it.

(3) Her Majesty may by Order in Council extend the power to grant interim relief conferred by subsection (1) so as to make it exercisable in relation to proceedings of any of the following descriptions, namely:

(a) proceedings commenced or to be commenced otherwise than in a Contracting State;

(b) proceedings whose subject-matter is not within the scope of the 1968 Convention as determined by Article 1;

(c) arbitration proceedings.

(4) An Order in Council under subsection (3):

(a) may confer power to grant only specified descriptions of interim relief;

(b) may make different provision for different classes of proceedings, for proceedings pending in different countries or courts outside the United Kingdom or in different parts of the United Kingdom, and for other different circumstances; and

(c) may impose conditions or restrictions on the exercise of any power conferred by the Order.

(5) An order in Council under subsection (3) which confers power to grant interim relief in relation to arbitration proceedings may provide for the repeal of any provision of section 12(6) of the Arbitration Act 1950 or section 21(1) of the Arbitration Act (Northern Ireland) 1937 to the extent that it is superseded by the provisions of the Order.

(6) Any Order in Council under subsection (3) shall be subject to annulment in pursuance of a resolution of either House of Parliament.

(7) In this section "interim relief", in relation to the High Court in England and Wales or Northern Ireland, means interim relief of any kind which that court has power to

grant in proceedings relating to matters within its jurisdiction, other than:
- (a) a warrant for the arrest of property; or
- (b) provision for obtaining evidence.

ARTICLE 1

This Convention shall apply in civil and commercial matters whatever the nature of the court or tribunal. It shall not extend, in particular, to revenue, customs or administrative matters.

The Convention shall not apply to:

(1) the status or legal capacity of natural persons, rights in property arising out of a matrimonial relationship, wills and succession;

(2) bankruptcy, proceedings relating to the winding-up of insolvent companies or other legal persons, judicial arrangements, compositions and analogous proceedings;

(3) social security;

(4) arbitration.

APPENDIX III
STATE IMMUNITY ACT 1978 c.33
SECTIONS 2–14

Exceptions from immunity

2.–(1) A state is not immune as respects proceedings in respect of which it has submitted to the jurisdiction of the courts of the United Kingdom.

(2) A State may submit after the dispute giving rise to the proceedings has arisen or by a prior written agreement; but a provision in any agreement that it is to be governed by the law of the United Kingdom is not to be regarded as a submission.

(3) A State is deemed to have submitted:
   (a) if it has instituted the proceedings; or
   (b) subject to subsections (4) and (5) below, if it has intervened or taken any step in the proceedings.

(4) Subsection (3)(b) above does not apply to intervention or any step taken for the purpose only of:
   (a) claiming immunity; or
   (b) asserting an interest in property in circumstances such that the State would have been entitled to immunity if the proceedings had been brought against it.

(5) Subsection (3)(b) above does not apply to any step taken by the State in ignorance of facts entitling it to immunity if those facts could not reasonably have been ascertained and immunity is claimed as soon as reasonably practicable.

(6) A submission in respect of any proceedings extends to any appeal but not to any counter-claim unless it arises out of the same legal relationship or facts as the claim.

(7) The head of a State's diplomatic mission in the United Kingdom, or the person for the time being performing his functions, shall be deemed to have authority to submit on behalf of the State in respect of any proceedings; and any person who has entered into a contract on behalf of and

with the authority of a State shall be deemed to have authority to submit on its behalf in respect of proceedings arising out of the contract.

3.–(1) A State is not immune as respect proceedings relating to:
    (a) a commercial transaction entered into by the State; or
    (b) an obligation of the State which by virtue of a contract (whether a commercial transaction or not) falls to be performed wholly or partly in the United Kingdom.

(2) This section does not apply if the parties to the dispute are States or have otherwise agreed in writing; and subsection (1)(b) above does not apply if the contract (not being a commercial transaction) was made in the territory of the State concerned and the obligation in question is governed by its administrative law.

(3) In this section "commerical transaction" means:
    (a) any contract for the supply of goods or services;
    (b) any loan or other transaction for the provision of finance and any guarantee or indemnity in respect of any such transaction or of any other financial obligation; and
    (c) any other transaction or activity (whether of a commercial, industrial, financial, professional or other similar character) into which a State enters or in which it engages otherwise than in the exercise of sovereign authority,

but neither paragraph of subsection (1) above applies to a contract of employment between a State and an individual.

4.–(1) A State is not immune as respects proceedings relating to a contract of employment between the State and an individual where the contract was made in the United Kingdom or the work is to be wholly or partly performed there.

(2) Subject to subsections (3) and (4) below, this section does not apply if:

(a) at the time when the proceedings are brought the individual is a national of the State concerned; or

(b) at the time when the contract was made the individual was neither a national of the United Kingdom nor habitually resident there; or

(c) the parties to the contract have otherwise agreed in writing.

(3) Where the work is for an office, agency or establishment maintained by the State in the United Kingdom for commercial purposes, subsection (2)(a) and (b) above do not exclude the application of this section unless the individual was, at the time when the contract was made, habitually resident in that State.

(4) Subsection (2)(c) above does not exclude the application of this section where the law of the United Kingdom requires the proceedings to be brought before a court of the United Kingdom.

(5) In subsection (2)(b) above "national of the United Kingdom" means a citizen of the United Kingdom and Colonies, a person who is a British subject by virtue of section 2, 13 or 16 of the British Nationality Act 1948 or by virtue of the British Nationality Act 1965, a British protected person within the meaning of the said Act of 1948 or a citizen of Southern Rhodesia.

(6) In this section "proceedings relating to a contract of employment" includes proceedings between the parties to such a contract in respect of any statutory rights or duties to which they are entitled or subject as employer or employee.

5. A State is not immune as respects proceedings in respect of:

(a) death or personal injury; or

(b) damage to or loss of tangible property,

caused by an act or omission in the United Kingdom.

6.–(1) A State is not immune as respects proceedings relating to:

    (a) any interest of the State in, or its possession or use of, immovable property in the United Kingdom; or

    (b) any obligation of the State, arising out of its interest in, or its possession or use of, any such property.

(2) A State is not immune as respects proceedings relating to any interest of the State in movable or immovable property, being an interest arising by way of succession, gift or *bona vacantia*.

(3) The fact that a State has or claims an interest in any property shall not preclude any court from exercising in respect of it any jurisdiction relating to the estates of deceased persons or persons of unsound mind or to insolvency, the winding up of companies or the administration of trusts.

(4) A court may entertain proceedings against a person other than a State notwithstanding that the proceedings relate to property:

    (a) which is in the possession or control of a State; or

    (b) in which a State claims an interest.

7. A State is not immune as respects proceedings relating to:

    (a) any patent, trade-mark, design or plant breeders' rights belonging to the State and registered or protected in the United Kingdom or for which the State has applied in the United Kingdom;

    (b) an alleged infringement by the State in the United Kingdom of any patent, trade-mark, design, plant breeders' rights or copyright; or

    (c) the right to use a trade or business name in the United Kingdom.

8.–(1) A State is not immune as respects proceedings relating to its membership of a body corporate, an unincorporated body or a partnership which:

(a) has members other than States; and

(b) is incorporated or constituted under the law of the United Kingdom or is controlled from or has its principal place of business in the United Kingdom,

being proceedings arising between the State and the body or its other members or, as the case may be, between the State and the other partners.

(2) This section does not apply if provision to the contrary has been made by an agreement in writing between the parties to the dispute or by the constitution or other instrument establishing or regulating the body or partnership in question.

9.–(1) Where a State has agreed in writing to submit a dispute which has arisen, or may arise, to arbitration, the State is not immune as respects proceedings in the courts of the United Kingdom which relate to the arbitration.

(2) This section has effect subject to any contrary provision in the arbitration agreement and does not apply to any arbitration agreement between States.

10.–(1) This section applies to:

(a) Admiralty proceedings; and

(b) proceedings on any claim which could be made the subject of Admiralty proceedings.

(2) A State is not immune as respects:

(a) an action *in rem* against a ship belonging to that State; or

(b) an action *in personam* for enforcing a claim in connection with such a ship,

if, at the time when the cause of action arose, the ship was in use or intended for use for commercial purposes.

(3) Where an action *in rem* is brought against a ship belonging to a State for enforcing a claim in connection with another ship belonging to that State, subsection (2)(a) above does not apply as respects the first-mentioned ship unless, at the time when the cause of action relating to the other

ship arose, both ships were in use or intended for use for commercial purposes.

(4) A State is not immune as respects:

    (a) an action *in rem* against a cargo belonging to that State if both the cargo and the ship carrying it were, at the time when the cause of action arose, in use or intended for use for commercial purposes; or

    (b) an action *in personam* for enforcing a claim in connection with such a cargo if the ship carrying it was then in use or intended for use as aforesaid.

(5) In the foregoing provisions references to a ship or cargo belonging to a State include references to a ship or cargo in its possession or control or in which it claims an interest; and, subject to subsection (4) above, subsection (2) above applies to property other than a ship as it applies to a ship.

(6) Sections 3 to 5 above do not apply to proceedings of the kind described in subsection (1) above if the State in question is a party to the Brussels Convention and the claim relates to the operation of a ship owned or operated by that State, the carriage of cargo or passengers or any such ship or the carriage of cargo owned by that State on any other ship.

11.–A State is not immune as respects proceedings relating to its liability for:

    (a) value added tax, any duty of customs or excise or any agricultural levy; or

    (b) rates in respect of premises occupied by it for commercial purposes.

PROCEDURE

12.–(1) Any writ or other document required to be served for instituting proceedings against a State shall be served by being transmitted through the Foreign and Commonwealth Office to the Ministry of Foreign Affairs of the State and service shall be deemed to have been effected when the writ or document is received at the Ministry.

(2) Any time for entering an appearance (whether pre-scribed by rules of court, or otherwise) shall begin to run two months after the date on which the writ or document is received as aforesaid.

(3) A State which appears in proceedings cannot thereafter object that subsection (1) above has not been complied with in the case of those proceedings.

(4) No judgment in default of appearance shall be given against a State except on proof that subsection (1) above has been complied with and that the time for entering an appearance as extended by subsection (2) above has expired.

(5) A copy of any judgment given against a State in default of appearance shall be transmitted through the Foreign and Commonwealth Office to the Ministry of Foreign Affairs of that State and any time for applying to have the judgment set aside (whether prescribed by rules of court or otherwise) shall begin to run two months after the date on which the copy of the judgment is received at the Ministry.

(6) Subsection (1) above does not prevent the service of a writ or other document in any manner to which the State has agreed and subsections (2) and (4) above do not apply where service is effected in any such manner.

(7) This section shall not be construed as applying to proceedings against a State by way of counter-claim or to an action *in rem*; and subsection (1) above shall not be construed as affecting any rules of court whereby leave is required for the service of process outside the jurisdiction.

13.–(1) No penalty by way of committal or fine shall be imposed in respect of any failure or refusal by or on behalf of a State to disclose or produce any document or other information for the purposes of proceedings to which it is a party.

(2) Subject to subsections (3) and (4) below:
    (a) relief shall not be given against a State by way of injunction or order for specific performance or for

the recovery of land or other property; and

(b) the property of a State shall not be subject to any process for the enforcement of a judgment or arbitration award or, in an action *in rem*, for its arrest, detention or sale.

(3) Subsection (2) above does not prevent the giving of any relief or the issue of any process with the written consent of the State concerned; and any such consent (which may be contained in a prior agreement) may be expressed so as to apply to a limited extent or generally; but a provision merely submitting to the jurisdiction of the courts is not to be regarded as a consent for the purposes of this subsection.

(4) Subsection (2)(b) above does not prevent the issue of any process in respect of property which is for the time being in use or intended for use for commercial purposes; but, in a case not falling with section 10 above, this subsection applies to property of a State party to the European Convention on State Immunity only if:

(a) the process is for enforcing a judgment which is final within the meaning of section 18(1)(b) below and the State has made a declaration under Article 24 of the Convention; or

(b) the process is for enforcing an arbitration award.

(5) The head of a State's diplomatic mission in the United Kingdom, or the person for the time being performing his functions, shall be deemed to have authority to give on behalf of the State any such consent as is mentioned in subsection (3) above and, for the purposes of subsection (4) above, his certificate to the effect that any property is not in use or intended for use by or on behalf of the State for commercial purposes shall be accepted as sufficient evidence of that fact unless the contrary is proved.

(6) In the application of this section to Scotland:

(a) the reference to "injunction" shall be construed as a reference to "interdict";

(b) for paragraph (b) of subsection (2) above there shall be substituted the following paragraph:

"(b) the property of a State shall not be subject to any diligence for enforcing a judgment or order of a court or a decree arbitral or, in an action *in rem*, to arrestment or sale."; and

(c) any reference to "process" shall be construed as a reference to "diligence", any reference to "the issue of any process" as a reference to "the doing of diligence" and the reference in subsection (4)(b) above to "an arbitration award" as a reference to a "decree arbitral".

SUPPLEMENTARY PROVISIONS

14.–(1) The immunities and privileges conferred by this Part of this Act apply to any foreign or commonwealth State other than the United Kingdom; and references to a State include references to:

(a) the sovereign or other head of that State in his public capacity;

(b) the government of that State; and

(c) any department of that government,

but not to any entity (hereafter referred to as a "separate entity") which is distinct from the executive organs of the government of the State and capable of suing or being sued.

(2) A separate entity is immune from the jurisdiction of the courts of the United Kingdom if, and only if:

(a) the proceedings relate to anything done by it in the exercise of sovereign authority; and

(b) the circumstances are such that a State (or, in the case of proceedings to which section 10 above applies, a State which is not a party to the Brussels Convention) would have been so immune.

(3) If a separate entity (not being a State's central bank or other monetary authority) submits to the jurisdiction in respect of proceedings in the case of which it is entitled to immunity by virtue of subsection (2) above, subsections (1) to (4) of section 13 above shall apply to it in respect of those

proceedings as if references to a State were references to that entity.

(4) Property of a State's central bank or other monetary authority shall not be regarded for the purposes of subsection (4) of section 13 above as in use or intended for use for commercial purposes; and where any such bank or authority is a separate entity subsections (1) and (3) of that section shall apply to it as if references to a State were references to the bank or authority.

(5) Section 12 above applies to proceedings against the constituent territories of a federal State; and Her Majesty may by Order in Council provide for the other provisions of this Part of this Act to apply to any such constituent territory specified in the Order as they apply to a State.

(6) Where the provisions of this Part of this Act do not apply to a constituent territory by virtue of any such Order subsections (2) and (3) above shall apply to it as if it were a separate entity.

APPENDIX IV
SUPREME COURT ACT 1981 c.54
SECTIONS 20–24

20.–(1) The Admiralty jurisdiction of the High Court shall be as follows, that is to say:

(a) jurisdiction to hear and determine any of the questions and claims mentioned in subsection (2);

(b) jurisdiction in relation to any of the proceedings mentioned in subsection (3);

(c) any other Admiralty jurisdiction which it had immediately before the commencement of this Act; and

(d) any jurisdiction connected with ships or aircraft which is vested in the High Court apart from this section and is for the time being by rules of court made or coming into force after the commencement of this Act assigned to the Queen's Bench Division and directed by the rules to be exercised by the Admiralty Court.

(2) The questions and claims referred to in subsection (1)(a) are:

(a) any claim to the possession or ownership of a ship or to the ownership of any share therein;

(b) any question arising between the co-owners of a ship as to possession, employment or earnings of that ship;

(c) any claim in respect of a mortgage of or charge on a ship or any share therein;

(d) any claim for damage received by a ship;

(e) any claim for damage done by a ship;

(f) any claim for loss of life or personal injury sustained in consequence of any defect in a ship or in her apparel or equivalent, or in consequence of the wrongful act, neglect or default of:

(i) the owners, charterers or persons in possession or control of a ship; or

(ii) the master or crew of a ship, or any other person for whose wrongful acts, neglects or defaults the owners, charterers of persons in possession or control of a ship are responsible,

being an act, neglect or default in the navigation or management of the ship, in the loading, carriage or discharge of goods on, in or from the ship, or in the embarkation, carriage or disembarkation of persons on, in or from the ship;

(g) any claim for loss of or damage to goods carried in a ship;

(h) any claim arising out of any agreement relating to the carriage of goods in a ship or to the use or hire of a ship;

(j) any claim into the nature of salvage (including any claim arising by virtue of the application, by or under section 51 of the Civil Aviation Act 1949, of the law relating to salvage to aircraft and their apparel and cargo);

(k) any claim in the nature of towage in respect of a ship or an aircraft;

(l) any claim in the nature of pilotage in respect of a ship or an aircraft;

(m) any claim in respect of goods or materials supplied to a ship for her operation or maintenance;

(n) any claim in respect of the construction, repair or equipment of a ship or in respect of dock charges or dues;

(o) any claim by a master or member of the crew of a ship for wages (including any sum allotted out of wages or adjudged by a superintendent to be due by way of wages);

(p) any claim by a master, shipper, charterer or agent in respect of disbursements made on account of a ship;

(q) any claim arising out of an act which is or is claimed to be a general average act;

(r) any claim arising out of bottomry;

(s) any claim for the forfeiture or condemnation of a ship or of goods which are being or have been carried, or have been attempted to be carried, in a ship, or for the restoration of a ship or any such goods after seizure, or for droits of Admiralty.

(3) The proceedings referred to in subsection (1)(b) are:

(a) any application to the High Court under the Merchant Shipping Acts 1894 to 1979 other than an application under section 55 of the Merchant Shipping Act 1894 for the appointment of a person to act as a substitute for a person incapable of acting;

(b) any action to enforce a claim for damage, loss of life or personal injury arising out of:

(i) a collision between ships; or

(ii) the carrying out of or omission to carry out a manoeuvre in the case of one or more of two or more ships; or

(iii) non-compliance, on the part of one or more of two or more ships, with the collision regulations;

(c) any action by shipowners or other persons under the Merchant Shipping Acts 1894 to 1979 for the limitation of the amount of their liability in connection with a ship or other property.

(4) The jurisdiction of the High Court under subsection (2)(b) includes power to settle any account outstanding and unsettled between the parties in relation to the ship, and to direct that the ship, or any share thereof, shall be sold, and to make such other order as the court thinks fit.

(5) Subsection (2)(e) extends to:

(a) any claim in respect of a liability incurred under the Merchant Shipping (Oil Pollution) Act 1971; and

(b) any claim in respect of a liability falling on the International Oil Pollution Compensation Fund under Part I of the Merchant Shipping Act 1974.

(6) The references in subsection (2)(j) to claims in the nature of salvage includes a reference to such claims for services rendered in saving life from a ship or an aircraft or

in preserving cargo, apparel or wreck as, under sections 544 to 546 of the Merchant Shipping Act 1894, or any Order in Council made under section 51 of the Civil Aviation Act 1949, are authorised to be made in connection with a ship or an aircraft.

(7) The preceding provisions of this section apply:

(a) in relation to all ships or aircraft, whether British or not and whether registered or not and wherever the residence or domicile of their owners may be;

(b) in relation to all claims, wherever arising (including in the case of cargo or wreck salvage, claims in respect of cargo or wreck found on land); and

(c) so far as they relate to mortgages and charges, to all mortgages or charges, whether registered or not and whether legal or equitable, including mortgages and charges created under foreign law:

Provided that nothing in this subsection shall be construed as extending the cases in which money or property is recoverable under any of the provisions of the Merchant Shipping Acts 1894 to 1979.

21.–(1) Subject to section 22, an action *in personam* may be brought in the High Court in all cases within the Admiralty jurisdiction of that court.

(2) In the case of any such claim as is mentioned in section 20(2)(a), (c) or (s) or any such question as is mentioned in section 20(2)(b), an action *in rem* may be brought in the High Court against the ship or property in connection with which the claim or question arises.

(3) In any case in which there is a maritime lein or other charge on any ship, aircraft or other property for the amount claimed, an action *in rem* may be brought in the High Court against that ship, aircraft or property.

(4) In the case of any such claim as is mentioned in section 20(2) (e) to (r), where:

(a) the claim arises in connection with a ship; and

(b) the person who would be liable on the claim in an

action *in personam* ("the relevant person") was, when the cause of action arose, the owner or charterer of, or in possession or in control of, the ship,

an action *in rem* may (whether or not the claim gives rise to a maritime lien on that ship) be brought in the High Court against:

(i) that ship, if at the time when the action is brought the relevant person is either the beneficial owner of that ship as respects all the shares in it or the charterer of it under a charter by demise; or

(ii) any other ship of which, at the time when the action is brought, the relevant person is the beneficial owner as respects all the shares in it.

(5) In the case of a claim in the nature of towage or pilotage in respect of an aricraft, an action *in rem* may be brought in the High Court against that aircraft if, at the time when the action is brought, it is beneficially owned by the person who would be liable on the claim in an action *in personam*.

(6) Where, in the exercise of its Admiralty jurisdiction, the High Court orders any ship, aircraft or other property to be sold, the court shall have jurisdiction to hear and determine any question arising as to the title to the proceeds of sale.

(7) In determining for the purposes of subsections (4) and (5) whether a person would be liable on a claim in an action *in personam* it shall be assumed that he has his habitual residence or a place of business within England or Wales.

(8) Where, as regards any such claim as is mentioned in section 20(2)(e) to (r), a ship has been served with a writ or arrested in an action *in rem* brought to enforce that claim, no other ship may be served with a writ or arrested in that or any other action *in rem* brought to enforce that claim; but this subsection does not prevent the issue, in respect of any one such claim, of a writ naming more than one ship or of two or more writs each naming a different ship.

22.–(1) This section applies to any claim for damage, loss

of life or personal injury arising out of:
  (a) a collision between ships; or
  (b) the carrying out of, or omission to carry out, a manoeuvre in the case of one or more of two or more ships; or
  (c) non-compliance, on the part of one or more of two or more ships, with the collision regulations.
(2) The High Court shall not entertain any action *in personam* to enforce a claim to which this section applies unless:
  (a) the defendant has his habitual residence or a place of business within England or Wales; or
  (b) the cause of action arose within inland waters of England or Wales or within the limits of a port of England and Wales; or
  (c) an action arising out of the same incident or series of incidents is proceeding in the court or has been heard and determined in the court.
In this subsection–

"inland waters" includes any part of the sea adjacent to the coast of the United Kingdom certified by the Secretary of State to be waters falling by international law to be treated as within the territorial sovereignty of Her Majesty apart from the operation of that law in relation to teritorial waters;

"port" means any port, harbour, river, estuary, haven, dock, canal or other place so long as a person or body of persons is empowered by or under an Act to make charges in respect of ships entering it or using the facilities therein, and "limits of a port" means the limits thereof as fixed by or under the Act in question or, as the case may be, by the relevant charges or custom;

"charges" means any charges with the exception of light dues, local light dues and any other charter in respect of lighthouses, buoys or beacons and of charges in respect of pilotage.

(3) The High Court shall not entertain any action *in personam* to enforce a claim to which this section applies until any proceedings previously brought by the plaintiff in any court outside England and Wales against the same defendant in respect of the same incident or series of incidents have been discontinued or otherwise come to an end.

(4) Subsections (2) and (3) shall apply to counterclaims (except counterclaims in proceedings arising out of the same incident or series of incidents) as they apply to actions, the references to the plaintiff and the defendant being for this purpose read as references to the plaintiff on the counterclaim and the defendant to the counterclaim respectively.

(5) Subsections (2) and (3) shall not apply to any action or counterclaim if the defendant thereto submits or has agreed to submit to the jurisdiction of the court.

(6) Subject to the provisions of subsection (3), the High Court shall have jurisdiction to entertain an action *in personam* to enforce a claim to which this section applies whenever any of the conditions specified in subsection (2)(a) to (c) is satisfied, and the rules of court relating to the service of process outside the jurisdiction shall make such provision as may appear to the rule-making authority to be appropriate having regard to the provisions of this subsection.

(7) Nothing in this section shall prevent an action which is brought in accordance with the provisions of this section in the High Court being transferred, in accordance with the enactments in that behalf, to some other court.

(8) For the avoidance of doubt it is hereby declared that this section applies in relation to the jurisdiction of the High Court not being Admiralty jurisdiction, as well as in relation to its Admiralty jurisdiction.

23.–The High Court shall not have jurisdiction to determine any claim or question certified by the Secretary of

State to be a claim or question which, under the Rhine Navigation Convention, falls to be determined in accordance with the provisions of that Convention; and any proceedings to enforce such a claim which are commenced in the High Court shall be set aside.

24.–(1) In sections 20 to 23 and this section, unless the context otherwise requires:

"Collision regulations" means regulations under section 4 of the Merchant Shipping Act 1894, or any such rules as are mentioned in section 421(1) of that Act or any rules made under section 421(2) of that Act;

"goods" includes baggage;

"master" has the same meaning as in the Merchant Shipping Act 1894, and accordingly includes every person (except a pilot) having command or charge of a ship.

"the Rhine Navigation Convention" means the Convention of the 7th October 1868 as revised by any subsequent Convention.

"towage" and "pilotage", in relation to an aircraft mean towage and pilotage while the aircraft is waterborne.

(2) Nothing in sections 20 to 23 shall:

(a) be construed as limiting the jurisdiction of the High Court to refuse to entertain an action for wages by the master or a member of the crew of a ship, not being a British ship;

(b) affect the provisions of section 552 of the Merchant Shipping Act 1894 (power of a receiver of wreck to detain a ship in respect of a salvage claim; or

(c) authorise proceedings *in rem*, in respect of any claim against the Crown, or the arrest, detention or sale of any of Her Majesty's ships or Her Majesty's aircraft or, subject to section 2(3) of the Hovercraft Act 1965 Her Majesty's hovercraft, or of any cargo or other property belonging to the Crown.

(3) In this section—

"Her Majesty's ships" and "Her Majesty's aircraft" have the meaning given by section 28(2) of the Crown Proceedings Act 1947;

"Her Majesty's hovercraft" means hovercraft belonging to the Crown in right of Her Majesty's Government in the United Kingdom or Her Majesty's Government in Northern Ireland.

INDEX